Editor-in-Chief and Founder:
 Lyndon H. LaRouche, Jr.
Editorial Board: *Lyndon H. LaRouche, Jr. , Helga
 Zepp-LaRouche, Robert Ingraham, Tony
 Papert, Gerald Rose, Dennis Small, Jeffrey
 Steinberg, William Wertz*
Co-Editors: *Robert Ingraham, Tony Papert*
Technology: *Marsha Freeman*
Transcriptions: *Katherine Notley*
Ebooks: *Richard Burden*
Graphics: *Alan Yue*
Photos: *Stuart Lewis*
Circulation Manager: *Stanley Ezrol*

INTELLIGENCE DIRECTORS
Economics: *Marcia Merry Baker, Paul Gallagher*
History: *Anton Chaitkin*
Ibero-America: *Dennis Small*
Russia and Eastern Europe: *Rachel Douglas*
United States: *Debra Freeman*

INTERNATIONAL BUREAUS
Bogotá: *Miriam Redondo*
Berlin: *Rainer Apel*
Copenhagen: *Tom Gillesberg*
Lima: *Sara Madueño*
Melbourne: *Robert Barwick*
Mexico City: *Gerardo Castilleja Chávez*
New Delhi: *Ramtanu Maitra*
Paris: *Christine Bierre*
Stockholm: *Ulf Sandmark*
United Nations, N.Y.C.: *Leni Rubinstein*
Washington, D.C.: *William Jones*
Wiesbaden: *Göran Haglund*

ON THE WEB
e-mail: eirns@larouchepub.com
www.larouchepub.com
www.executiveintelligencereview.com
www.larouchepub.com/eiw
Webmaster: *John Sigerson*
Assistant Webmaster: *George Hollis*
Editor, Arabic-language edition: *Hussein Askary*

EIR (ISSN 0273-6314) *is published weekly
(50 issues), by EIR News Service, Inc.,
P.O. Box 17390, Washington, D.C. 20041-0390.
(703) 297-8434*

European Headquarters: E.I.R. GmbH, Postfach
Bahnstrasse 9a, D-65205, Wiesbaden, Germany
Tel: 49-611-73650
Homepage: http://www.eir.de
e-mail: info@eir.de
Director: Georg Neudecker

Montreal, Canada: 514-461-1557
eir@eircanada.ca

Denmark: EIR - Denmark, Sankt Knuds Vej 11,
basement left, DK-1903 Frederiksberg, Denmark.
Tel.: +45 35 43 60 40, Fax: +45 35 43 87 57. e-mail:
eirdk@hotmail.com.

Mexico City: EIR, Sor Juana Inés de la Cruz 242-2
Col. Agricultura C.P. 11360
Delegación M. Hidalgo, México D.F.
Tel. (5525) 5318-2301
eirmexico@gmail.com

History and the Midterm Elections

History and the Midterm Elections

Aug. 20—On the one side, there are those rarer moments of history when brains and guts can win the battle to uplift man and his condition far into the future. On the other side, in the decades and centuries between those rare moments, you fight anyway; you never stop. But what you win at these times, rather than immediate victories, is the preparation of the forces which will win the war of the future.

The period since the Presidential election, particularly this Autumn, constitutes one of those rarer moments.

EIR's founder, the great economist Lyndon LaRouche, responded to the first reports of Donald Trump's election victory in November 2016, by indicating that the rejection of Hillary Clinton, Barack Obama and their forty thieves, was much more than a U.S. event. It was the world as a whole which had repudiated them—not just Americans who were so fed up with this bunch that they couldn't bear to look at them again.

The larger historical context of that 2016 election result, which inspires our knowledge of real meaning of the November 2018 midterm elections, is the subject of articles by William Wertz and Lyndon LaRouche in this issue.

To try to encapsulate it here, it resembles the closure of the long cycle of history which began April 12, 1945, the day of Franklin Roosevelt's untimely death. Through his policies, he had taken us out of the Great Depression. At the same time, he had launched the same New Deal policies throughout the Western Hemisphere in the form of his Good Neighbor policy. The financial side of the Good Neighbor policy was an international credit system, not a monetary system, aimed at economic development, industrialization, and raising the standard of living. It was to be run multilaterally by perfectly sovereign nation-states through a proposed Inter-American Bank.

On April 12, 1945, World War II was drawing to a close. Europe and much of Asia had been destroyed, while the United States, with its wartime economic mobilization, had become the greatest productive power the world had ever seen. Around the world, regardless of nation or party, the survivors of that terrible war, almost without exception, looked to the United States and Franklin Roosevelt to lead them to a permanent peace, to reconstruction of the destroyed nations, and to freedom and economic development for the British Empire's colonies and semi-colonies of Africa, Asia and the Americas.

For them, only that kind of future could possibly redeem the horrors of that war.

Franklin Roosevelt's design for the postwar world credit system, which became the Bretton Woods system, modelled itself on the credit system of his Good Neighbor Policy—and the architects of the latter, especially Harry Dexter White, were then the architects of the original Bretton Woods institutions. Thus, Roosevelt proposed an international credit system—not a monetary system—which would enable yesterday's colonized peoples, now independent sovereign nations, to industrialize and develop advanced full-set economies. Fixed exchange rates, unlike the floating-exchange casino of today, would make large-scale long-term, very-low interest development loans possible, facilitating massive capital exports from the United States, and then other nations, to develop former colonies and semi-colonies.

The alliance of Roosevelt's "Big Four," the United States, Russia, China, and the difficult ally Great Britain, was to be the keystone of the new world credit system, as of the new United Nations Organization.

Roosevelt pushed this program through in the teeth of bitter opposition from the British Empire represented by Winston Churchill and John Maynard Keynes, and from the American anglophiles, our Tories, especially on Wall Street. Churchill needed Roosevelt to win the war, but as soon that was ensured, he wanted him and his policies overthrown and destroyed the day after.

These enemies began to move rapidly to undercut Roosevelt after Normandy, and then, when Churchill's dupe Truman replaced the deceased Roosevelt in April 1945, Roosevelt's policies and personnel were shown the door. Churchill launched the Cold War to destroy Roosevelt's Big Four alliance. Instead of keeping the war-industries running, while changing them over for massive capital exports to industrialize "underdeveloped" countries, as Roosevelt had wished, Truman shut them down.

Since April 12, 1945, with the partial exception of the 1000 days of Jack Kennedy, we have been speeding ever more rapidly downwards. On Aug. 15, 1971, Richard Nixon exploded what remained of the fixed-rate Bretton Woods system, opening the door to today's floating currencies, which feed speculation and hamper development. Since the Oil Hoax of 1973, the dollar—the so-called Eurodollar—has been created and run from London, with no regulation from the United States. In 1989, Britain's Margaret Thatcher dictated that the breakdown of the Soviet and East European system would not be used for a higher East-West integration for joint development, as Lyndon LaRouche proposed, but that Eastern Europe and the former Soviet Union would instead be given over to an orgy of looting.

In 1999, after being tamed by impeachment, Bill Clinton acceded to the revocation of Roosevelt's Glass-Steagall Act.

Over the turn of the current century, we have gone from Bill Clinton to much worse—to Cheney's puppet "Dubya" Bush, and then the Satanic Obama.

Our factories have closed; homelessness and drug addiction are everywhere. There is no question but that Americans had suffered under a "long train of abuses" before daring to reject Wall Street and the corrupt establishment of both parties to elect Donald Trump. But this would not have happened without Lyndon LaRouche's long fight to re-establish Hamiltonian principles of economy, and continue the Roosevelt revolution from a higher and more advanced standpoint.

Meanwhile, the Russians have gone through their own kind of Hell. Russians say their country suffered more under Thatcher's looting than even in World War II, as life-expectancy and population plummeted. But then, since 1999 (preceded by the brief premiership of Yevgeny Primakov), Vladimir Putin has done the unbelievable to drag Russia out of the dungheap which Margaret Thatcher had made of it. A new, viable, leadership has arisen there.

During a longer period in China, the destructive legacy of the Maoist Cultural Revolution and earlier Great Leap Forward policies had been overturned under the leadership of Deng Xiaoping and his successors since 1978. They have based themselves ever more clearly on the Chinese classics of Confucius, Mencius and the later Zhu Xi. As *EIR*'s Michael Billington has shown, in his taking up Gottfried Leibniz's work of the 17th and 18th centuries, these Chinese classics are in coherence with the Christian humanism of the Renaissance which underlay American policies from Benjamin Franklin to Franklin Roosevelt. Now, Deng Xiaoping's successor Xi Jinping, President of China since 2013, has taken up a mission of world development whose vision was launched by Lyndon and Helga LaRouche in the 1990s—the Eurasian Land-Bridge, also called the New Silk Road and the Belt and Road Initiative.

Neither the Russian nor the Chinese development would have occurred without the ideas of Lyndon LaRouche, spread by his many trips to Russia, his wife's trips to China, by LaRouche students in both countries who translated his works, and in other ways. All these years, as the world and U.S. situations deteriorated, LaRouche was fighting fiercely—but apparently losing every fight, or almost every fight. The same Robert Mueller who is now trying to overthrow the U.S. President and Constitution, had LaRouche railroaded, falsely convicted, and imprisoned for five years, on behalf of London. LaRouche was losing every fight— or so it seemed until now.

Now, what Churchill destroyed in the late 1940s is back on the agenda again today. In the leadership of today's Russia and China, there is the willingness to reconstitute Roosevelt's Big Four, not only for peace, but for a world credit system along Roosevelt's intentions: LaRouche's "New Bretton Woods System." Britain as the fourth member was forced on Roosevelt by the difficult wartime alliance. For the fourth member today, LaRouche has long specified India—which Roosevelt would have included, but could not, because it was still a colony in 1945.

Of course, none of this works without a central role by the United States. But this is precisely what President Trump is prepared to do—and what his two predecessors fiercely opposed. No wonder that former President Obama is the "field marshal" for the British in trying to bring down this U.S. Presidency. Or do you think it's a coincidence that the leading Americans in this evil effort are all Obama's former subordinates?

All this indicates what we must fight *for* in this election period. What we must fight against is the threatened impeachment of this President, which would destroy all these prospects, and doom us to chaos and near-term war, facing nuclear war down the road.

On impeachment—don't be a fool! Face the reality that a majority-Democratic House of Representatives will quickly vote to impeach this President on a strict party-line vote, regardless of whatever better judgment any of those Democratic Representatives may hold in private. Unfortunately, any Democratic Representative today considers himself or herself completely powerless in the face of the blackmail and other power wielded by Obama, Hillary Clinton and the other mad dogs. By all means, Democrats should be elected to Congress if they're *good*—but they are *not* good unless they sign— and adhere to—the pledge offered by the LaRouche PAC campaign, which says, "I will not support impeachment of President Donald Trump. In general, I will act to end the on-going insurrection against the President and to investigate those responsible, referring them for prosecution where warranted." Otherwise, no citizen should cast his or her vote for a Democratic congressional candidate in this election.

Impeachment will be the first punch in a campaign to obstruct, tie down and destroy this President. But don't delude yourself that if somehow he is removed, we'll return to the days of Obama. Not at all! Haven't you noticed how much worse Obama, and his stooges Hillary, Brennan, Comey, Clapper and company are now, than they ever were in office? How much more contemptuous of the law? How they are a thousand times more eager for war than ever before?

It's the British Empire. The British Empire is in conniptions because their prisoners have escaped, or are in process of escaping. If they get their way, they'll make sure it never happens again. Not just through a police state, but through war. War was always the means they used to control the United States and make it impotent. Elect a Democratic majority which has not signed the pledge above, and you're on a very short path to impeachment and war.

But, more important—This, then, is the great opportunity we face. For the first time since Jack Kennedy and Franklin Roosevelt before him, we have a President who is fully committed both to peace and to economic development. Among the election promises which he is working to fulfill are creating productive, well-paying jobs for Americans, and rebuilding American infrastructure. We must convince and support President Trump to introduce the current version of the Roosevelt recovery program, found in Lyndon LaRouche's Four New Laws of June 2014, which also include the restoration of Glass-Steagall, which the President supports. We must convince and support President Trump to join with Russia, China and India, to launch a new world credit system to replace the bankrupt speculative system which exploded in 2008. All or virtually all other nations will willingly sign on.

EIR Contents

www.larouchepub.com   Volume 45, Number 34, August 24, 2018

Public Domain

**Cover
This Week**

*Franklin D.
Roosevelt and
Winston Churchill
brief war
correspondents
during the
Casablanca
Conference,
French Morocco,
January 24, 1943.*

HISTORY AND THE MIDTERM ELECTIONS

2 EDITORIAL
History and the Midterm Elections

I. Our Task in 2018

6 IN THE FOOTSTEPS OF FDR
A New Bretton Woods System
by William Wertz

13 ZEPP-LAROUCHE WEBCAST
As Financial System Teeters, Four Power Agreement for a New Bretton Woods Is the Solution

II. America's Pacific Mission

21 **America-China Relations: The Longer View**
by William Jones

III. LaRouche's New Bretton Woods

34 **New Bretton Woods: Russia's Role in a Recovery**
by Lyndon H. LaRouche, Jr.
August 20, 2008

72 PETITION
The Leaders of the United States, Russia, China, and India Must Take Action!

74 EDITORIAL
Will Brennan Be Called Before a Grand Jury?
by Harley Schlanger

IN THE FOOTSTEPS OF FDR

A New Bretton Woods System

by William Wertz

The following is an edited transcript of the opening remarks, by William Wertz, to LaRouche PAC's weekly Fireside Chat on Thursday, Aug. 16, 2018. The full video is available here.

I want to give you more of a sense of President Franklin Roosevelt's original intention in forming the Bretton Woods system. This was the system that was put together at a conference in Bretton Woods, New Hampshire in 1944. There's a very interesting book, which Tony Papert, who's the co-editor of *Executive Intelligence Review*, lent me, called *Forgotten Foundations of Bretton Woods: International Development and the Making of the Postwar Order*. That book may be very helpful to many of you who want to further study that conference and its impact.

The Schiller Institute is circulating a petition internationally, addressed to the leaders of the United States, Russia, China and India, which begins, "We, the undersigned, appeal to President Trump, President Putin, President Xi Jinping and Prime Minister Modi, to convoke an emergency summit in order to create a New Bretton Woods global monetary system." I urge people to sign and circulate that petition.

Lyndon LaRouche, on November 11, 2008, presented remarks to a meeting in Washington, D.C. which were published in *EIR* under the title, Only My Reforms Can Save the Planet from a Dark Age. This was is in 2008, as the financial crisis had just broken out. He called for a Four Power agreement to create a New Bretton Woods system. He notably stated:

So, if we create this seed crystal, of these four nations, and others who join them, we now can have, any time we decide to do it—if the President of the United States says, to the President of Russia and to the President of China, and to the government of India, and some other countries: "Let's make this agreement!", the United States has Constitutionally, the Constitutional apparatus and the authority, to do this!

This idea which we're putting forward now, really is

The Mount Washington Hotel & Resort

U.S. Treasury Secretary Henry Morgenthau opens the Bretton Woods International Monetary Conference at the Mount Washington Hotel in New Hampshire, July 1, 1944.

the critical solution to the ongoing crisis in the world today. And it's very interesting, because the old Bretton Woods system, created by Franklin Roosevelt, before the end of World War II, reflects the ideas of the American System, the ideas of Alexander Hamilton. Franklin Roosevelt, when he was at Harvard, wrote his thesis on Alexander Hamilton and his great-great grandfather, Isaac Roosevelt, who was a direct collaborator with Alexander Hamilton in Manhattan at the time of the founding of the country.

What Roosevelt represented was the American System of Alexander Hamilton and the American System of Abraham Lincoln. The Bretton Woods system was essentially an extension of his Good Neighbor Policy towards Ibero-America.

Roosevelt and Churchill brief war correspondents during the Casablanca Conference, French Morocco, January 24, 1943.

The basic idea is expressed most clearly in a book by FDR's son, Elliott Roosevelt, entitled *As He Saw It.* Elliott Roosevelt accompanied Franklin Roosevelt to a number of the major conferences which took place during World War II, including those between Franklin Roosevelt and Winston Churchill. I want to give you a sense of what was at stake in World War II, with focus on the clash between Franklin Roosevelt and Churchill, which was the clash between the American System of Alexander Hamilton and the British Empire—the Anglo-Dutch system being defended by Winston Churchill.

As Father Saw It

I'm going to read two sections from this book, because it gets really to the core of the issue which is before us today. Elliott Roosevelt writes as follows:

> It must be remembered that at this time Churchill was the war leader, Father only the president of a state which had indicated its sympathies in a tangible fashion. Thus, Churchill still arrogated the conversational lead, still dominated the after-dinner hours. But the difference was beginning to be felt.
>
> And it was evidenced first, sharply, over Empire.
>
> Father started it.

"Of course," he remarked, with a sly sort of assurance, "of course, after the war, one of the preconditions of any lasting peace will have to be the greatest possible freedom of trade."

He paused. The P.M.'s head was lowered; he was watching Father steadily, from under one eyebrow.

"No artificial barriers," Father pursued. "As few favored economic agreements as possible. Opportunities for expansion. Markets open for healthy competition." His eye wandered innocently around the room.

Churchill shifted in his armchair. "The British Empire trade agreements" he began heavily, "are—"

Father broke in. "Yes. Those Empire trade agreements are a case in point. It's because of them that the people of India and Africa, of all the colonial Near East and Far East, are still as backward as they are."

Churchill's neck reddened and he crouched forward. "Mr. President, England does not propose for a moment to lose its favored position among the British Dominions. The trade that has made England great shall continue, and under conditions prescribed by England's ministers."

"You see," said Father slowly, "it is along in here somewhere that there is likely to be some disagreement between you, Winston, and me.

"I am firmly of the belief that if we are to arrive at a stable peace it must involve the development of backward countries. Backward peoples. How can this be done? It can't be done, obviously, by eighteenth-century methods. Now—"

"Who's talking eighteenth-century methods?"

"Whichever of your ministers recommends a policy which takes wealth in raw materials out of a colonial country, but which returns nothing to the people of that country in consideration. *Twentieth*-century methods involve bringing industry to these colonies. *Twentieth*-century methods include increasing the wealth of a people by increasing their standard of living, by educating them, by bringing them sanitation— by making sure that they get a return for the raw wealth of their community."

Around the room, all of us were leaning forward attentively. Hopkins was grinning. Commander Thompson, Churchill's aide, was looking glum and alarmed. The P.M. himself was beginning to look apoplectic.

"You mentioned India," he growled.

"Yes. I can't believe that we can fight a war against fascist slavery, and at the same time not work to free people all over the world from a backward colonial policy."

"What about the Philippines?"

"I'm glad you mentioned them. They get their independence, you know, in 1946. And they've gotten modern sanitation, modern education; their rate of illiteracy has gone steadily down...."

"There can be no tampering with the Empire's economic agreements."

"They're artificial ..."

"They're the foundation of our greatness."

"The peace," said Father firmly, "cannot include any continued despotism. The structure of the peace demands and will get equality of peoples. Equality of peoples involves the utmost freedom of competitive trade. Will anyone suggest that Germany's attempt to dominate trade in central Europe was not a major contributing factor to war?"

It was an argument that could have no resolution between these two men....

A Dead Duck

The conversation resumed the following evening, as Elliott Roosevelt reports:

Gradually, very gradually, and very quietly, the mantle of leadership was slipping from British shoulders to American. We saw it when, late in the evening, there came one flash of the argument that had held us hushed the night before. In a sense, it was to be the valedictory of Churchill's outspoken Toryism, as far as Father was concerned. Churchill had got up to walk about the room. Talking, gesticulating, at length he paused in front of Father, was silent for a moment, looking at him, and then brandished a stubby forefinger under Father's nose.

"Mr. President," he cried, "I believe you are trying to do away with the British Empire. Every idea you entertain about the structure of the postwar world demonstrates it. But in spite of that"— and his forefinger waved—"in spite of that, we know that you constitute our only hope. And"— his voice sank dramatically—"*you* know that *we* know it. *You* know that *we* know that without America, the Empire won't stand."

Churchill admitted, in that moment, that he knew the peace could only be won according to precepts which the United States of America would lay down. And in saying what he did, he was acknowledging that British colonial policy would be a dead duck, and British attempts to dominate world trade would be a dead duck, and British ambitions to play off the U.S.S.R. against the U.S.A. would be a dead duck.

Or would have been, if Father had lived.

Eighteenth-Century Methods

And that right there, is the fundamental conflict in the world to this day. This goes back—and this is important to recognize—this goes 250 years, approximately, to 1763, which was the year in which Europe's Seven Years War, which we, in the United States, call the French and Indian War, was settled in the Treaty of Paris. That settlement essentially handed over India to the British East India Company. The American Revolution was to be fought against the British Empire. During the Boston Tea Party, the three ships that had brought tea from China were, in fact, ships of the British East India Company.

Painting by William Walcutt

Pulling down the statue of King George III in New York City in 1776.

By 1773 the British had vastly expanded their control of India, and they were already beginning their increased export of opium from India to China. The Boston Tea Party was 1773. The Declaration of Independence was 1776; the U.S. Constitution was signed in 1787. By 1803, at the height of the British East India Company's control of India, that company had a private army of 260,000 troops. Let us not forget that Russia had backed the American Revolution as a leading member of the League of Armed Neutrality.

The British East India Company, going back approximately 250 years, was the enemy of United States at its inception and was the enemy of India, which that company had, in fact, taken over. The Company committed genocide by destroying agriculture in order to grow opium which that same Company then forced, through wars, the Chinese to consume.

So you have China, India, the United States, all direct enemies of the British East India Company and this Anglo-Dutch imperial system, while Russia at that time backed the nascent United States through the League of Armed Neutrality. Later Russia backed the United States in the Civil War, when it sent ships to New York City and San Francisco in order to prevent any kind of British military intervention on behalf of the Confederacy.

So the Four Powers have been, in a certain sense, united against the British Empire going all way back to the 1760s.

Roosevelt's Original Concept

Let's now look at the original Bretton Woods agreement. It was really quite extraordinary—Roosevelt said that the concept was based on his Good Neighbor Policy toward Ibero-America. The model for what became the Bretton Woods system was a proposal for an Inter-American Bank in 1939-1940 that never was implemented because it wasn't ratified by the United States. So this bank is really extraordinary. Here are some of the ideas of the draft bylaws of this bank. The bank was to—

Facilitate the prudent investment of funds to stimulate the full productive use of capital and credit.

Promote the development of industry, public utilities, mining, agriculture, commerce and finance in the Western Hemisphere.

Foster cooperation among the American republics in the field of agriculture, industry, public utilities, mining, marketing, commerce, transportation and related economic and financial matters.

Encourage and promote research in the technology of agriculture, industry, public utilities, mining, and commerce.

The key person with whom Roosevelt worked to create this bank was Harry Dexter White, who was also involved in the New Deal. And in a certain sense, the Bretton Woods for the post-World War II period was an effort to internationalize the New Deal, to have projects like the Tennessee Valley Authority throughout the world, and to develop the world.

Roosevelt versus Keynes

There was a contrary view of the Bretton Woods system, which was that of John Maynard Keynes, the representative of the British Empire at the Bretton Woods conference. And of course, John Maynard Keynes' economic theories are pretty well known. The best example is the idea that all you have to do is try to facilitate consumption; there is no such thing as productive investment versus nonproductive. You can hire somebody to dig a hole and hire somebody else to fill the hole; somebody else to cover the hole, and then somebody else to uncover the hole. There is nothing productive: You're paying people and therefore, they consume, but there's never any explanation as to how what they're consuming is produced. That's John Maynard Keynes. He fought on behalf of the Empire at the Bretton Woods conference.

The original Bretton Woods system was very interesting. We still have institutions created at that conference—the International Monetary Fund (IMF) and the World Bank, which was initially called the International Bank for Reconstruction and Development. Two of the principles behind FDR's original mission for the

IMF

Harry Dexter White (left) and John Maynard Keynes, at the inaugural meeting of the IMF's board of governors in Savannah, Georgia, March 8, 1946.

International Bank for Reconstruction and Development were "encouraging development of productive facilities and resources in less-developed countries" and the "provision of long-term capital for desirable, productive projects that serve directly or indirectly to permanently raise the standard of living of the borrowing country."

Two of the key conditions for the credit that would be extended by International Bank for Reconstruction and Development were that the interest rate could not be excessive—and we have just learned that this credit was to be long-term capital for productive projects so it has to be productive investment—and that credit could not be for the purpose of repayment of an old loan.

That is very important and the abandonment of that principle became starkly manifest after Nixon took the dollar off the gold-reserve standard and introduced the floating exchange rate in 1971. The World Bank and the IMF in that period began to impose austerity conditions on all countries, and almost all loans extended were used to repay old loans. Nothing was put into productive projects like the TVA. Instead, the World Bank became an advocate of what it called appropriate technologies, which are essentially technologies that can be implemented on a village level. So you never get out of poverty.

FDR's Many Partners

The further point about the Bretton Woods conference is that it was international. Before the BRICS, before the Shanghai Cooperation Organization and the Eurasian Economic Union, there was Roosevelt's Bretton Woods.

At the Bretton Woods conference, there was representation from 19 Ibero-American countries—all but Argentina. There were four African countries: Egypt, Ethiopia, Liberia, and South Africa. There were five Asian countries: China, India, Iran, Iraq, and the Philippines—East and West Asia. There were four countries from Eastern Europe: the then Czechoslovakia, Greece, Poland, and Yugoslavia.

John Maynard Keynes addresses the Bretton Woods Conference, July 4, 1944.

Thirty-two of the 44 nations attending were developing countries (sometimes called "undeveloped countries").

The second-largest delegation was from China. The United States had a delegation of 45; China had a delegation of 33; Brazil, which is a member of the BRICS today, had 13; Cuba, ten; and India, eight. Now the problem with India at that point was that it was still a British colony, so of the eight representatives, some were from the Congress Party, but others were from Britain, so that delegation was split. There were eight representatives from Peru; nine from Chile; eight from Poland, and seven from Mexico.

Mexico played a really critical role in the Bretton Woods conference. There were three commissions at the conference. Harry Dexter White, FDR's representative, addressed one; Keynes addressed a second one; and a representative of the Mexican delegation addressed the third.

This was a full commitment to doing what China is now doing, and what the BRICS are attempting to do now. This was Roosevelt's policy. China, then, strongly supported the FDR policy. Sun Yat Sen had been educated in Hawaii, and was educated in the American System—he had put forward a proposal for international development in 1921, before his death in 1925.

The United States worked closely with China and India—although that was complicated by the fact that the Brits still controlled India as a colony—and with Brazil, now a member of the BRICS; South Africa, now a member of the BRICS; Mexico; and eastern European countries notably including Yugoslavia, which later became a founding member of the Non-Aligned Movement after World War II.

This is what America at that point represented. But as soon as Roosevelt was dead, there were efforts to change this. Those efforts weren't immediately successful. Once Nixon took the dollar off the gold-reserve system and introduced floating exchange rates—free trade, globalization, outsourcing, and the ideology of a so-called post-industrial society become predominant from that point on.

Lyndon LaRouche has consistently advocated returning to Roosevelt's conception at that Bretton Woods conference. In a certain sense, we now see a new situation developing in the world today. The Eurasian nations have moved on a course to eliminate poverty, to

IMF Managing Director Christine Lagarde is shown a mobile solar kiosk at kLab in Kigali, Rwanda, Jan. 28, 2015.

develop underdeveloped countries, through nuclear energy, through high-speed rail, through water projects and so forth. They've created certain banks in order to facilitate that, like the New Development Bank (NDB) of the BRICS, and the Asian Infrastructure Investment Bank (AIIB).

We still have this huge, bankrupt trans-Atlantic system that is threatening to explode the entire world economy. With floating exchange rates, we have massive speculation in currencies.

Re-Unite the Adversaries of the Empire

We are at a point, if we're going to resolve the differences among nations, we need to eliminate globalization, eliminate free trade, and eliminate the idea of a post-industrial society. We need to have a New Bretton Woods—to forge an agreement among these four nations that were involved—going back over 250 years for each of these four countries—in the fight against the British East India Company and the British Empire, and that were all involved, to one degree or another, in the effort with Roosevelt to create the original Bretton Woods system, which was then later destroyed by Nixon and his advisors, like George Shultz.

The effort now is to bring those four countries together, to defeat this British monetarist ideology, which is the means by which they exercise empire. Lyndon LaRouche proposed going back to a gold-reserve system, and reintroducing fixed exchange rates. The kinds of projects you need to have in the world may take 25 or 50 years to have their full effect, in terms of

President Trump could say to President Putin, President Xi, and Prime Minister Modi: "Let's make a deal." Here, Presidents Putin, Trump, Quang, and Xi on a walk-about together at the Asia-Pacific Economic Cooperation Vietnam 2017 Summit.

increases in productivity, both in developed countries, such as the United States, and in the developing countries. These development projects will require gearing up our industry, creating millions of higher-paid, skilled jobs in the United States, for capital goods exports to develop the underdeveloped countries, as well as developing our own infrastructure.

We would be working with China, with Russia, with India, and other countries that join—Japan would join. We might even bring some sense to European countries which have essentially given up their sovereignty with the European Union.

We would actually be able to pull the world together in terms of the development orientation which Roosevelt had intended and which the world desperately needs. The irony is that everything today that the Chinese are doing, that the Russians are doing, and that the Indians are doing with the BRICS, and is being done with the One Belt One Road, is what Roosevelt intended at the end of World War II. But it was thwarted after his death by Churchill, by Truman and others.

In this last stretch before the U.S. midterm elections, it is not just a question of defeating the coup against President Trump, we have to create the circumstances, in defeating that coup, in which President Trump can reach out and do now what Lyndon LaRouche proposed back in 2008. President Trump can say to President Putin, President Xi, and Prime Minister Modi, "Let's make an agreement." Trump might actually say, "Let's make a deal."

But the deal is for humanity. It's a concept of all humanity, through the efforts of these four critical countries, ending empire, and creating the conditions under which the world as a whole is oriented toward its common destiny, which is to develop the productive powers and the well-being—the general welfare on a global scale—of all humanity.

And that is the best thing that can be done for our country: We will then revitalize industry and revitalize our agriculture. We will be doing that through a policy of economic development and that will bring peace, as opposed to regime change.

Let us remember, the other aspect of the British and this British Imperial system is genocide, and I think that it is really critical that people understand that. The British have committed greater genocide throughout the world perhaps than anybody—they've committed multiple genocides in India. The royal family's Prince Philip has said that when he dies, he would like to be reincarnated as a deadly virus so he can reduce the world's population. That's the mentality of the British system.

There's no value placed on human creativity, human productivity, human life. It is entirely a bestial conception of mankind: Keeping man down, don't let him develop his creative powers. Get him on drugs—in China it was opium. Look at the United States today in terms of drugs; look at Mexico in terms of the destruction of the population by drugs. That's the British policy. And that is what has to be defeated.

We have to unite Russia, China, India, and the United States against this Anglo-Dutch liberal system, against the British Empire, and on behalf of the principle of the American System, which was embedded in the original Bretton Woods. We have to revive that globally. And that's the basic message I want to convey.

As Financial System Teeters, Four Power Agreement for a New Bretton Woods Is the Solution

This is the edited transcript of the Schiller Institute's New Paradigm webcast of August 17, 2018, an interview with the founder of the Schiller Institutes, Helga Zepp-LaRouche. She was interviewed by Harley Schlanger. A video *of the webcast is available.*

Harley Schlanger: Hello, I'm Harley Schlanger with the Schiller Institute. Welcome to this week's webcast with our founder, Helga Zepp-LaRouche.

The Schiller Institute has just drafted a new petition calling for an emergency summit among four powers, the United States, Russia, China, and India, to create a New Bretton Woods. This is something that is urgently needed: The current financial system is in terrible shape. It's not just one problem—it's not just Turkey or Argentina—it's the whole system. This comes at a time when there's a political crisis in the world with the continuation of Russiagate in the United States. So, it's absolutely crucial that steps be taken to address the financial crisis—the most important step would be a conference for a New Bretton Woods agreement. Our listeners and viewers should read the petition titled, "The Leaders of the United States, Russia, China and India Must Take Action!" and circulate it.

Helga, why don't you give people a sense of what's in that petition and the thinking behind it?

Why a New International Monetary Conference?

Helga Zepp-LaRouche: I think most people would agree that the world is a complete mess. You have many

Lyndon LaRouche's newspaper, September 1, 1971.

different problems. You have the immediate danger of a new financial blowout. There are analysts warning that there are storms over the United States, that you could have a complete financial collapse way before the midterm elections. We also have the emerging markets reverse-carry-trade problem that is hitting Turkey and Argentina, but possibly other nations. There is also the refugee crisis and the collapse of infrastructure, as the collapse of the bridge in Genoa demonstrates. The EU is in a state of disarray and the demographic curve in the United States is collapsing. Add to that the virtually unbelievable yearly figures of deaths by opiate overdoses in the United States.

Most people, in the face of these—and I could probably make a longer list—would most probably say, "How can you remedy all of these things? There seems to be no solution. How can we possibly be in a safe world?" I think there is a common thread of action, which will not remedy everything at once, but it will begin the process of putting the world back in order, so that we can start solving all of these problems.

I think that the reference point of when the Western financial system went haywire is what needs to be understood. My husband, the American economist and statesman Lyndon LaRouche, is probably the only economist who, when it happened, put his finger absolutely on the problem, namely when President Nixon, on August 15, 1971, cancelled the fixed exchange rate system of the Bretton Woods system, decoupled the dollar from gold, and started monetarist, neo-liberal policies. My husband, (at that point he was not my husband yet) said the world now faces a stark choice: If we continue this monetarist neo-liberal policy, sooner or later there will be another great depression, another danger of fascism—or the world will establish a just new world economic system.

He was absolutely on the mark saying that, and ever since, he has been absolutely consistently right in every economic prognosis. He forecast the 1987 crash. One week before the secondary mortgage crisis in the United States started to detonate—what became the 2007-2008 Lehman Brothers/AIG bankruptcy, the big systemic crisis of 2008—he made a video address in which he said that this system is gone and all you will see now are the different symptoms coming to the surface. He also made the point emphatically that the condition of American infrastructure was terrible, and there be would be collapses. Exactly one week later, the bridge in Minneapolis, Minnesota came down taking scores of commuters with it.

Over the years, my husband has repeatedly called for a reestablishment of the New Bretton Woods system, to go back to Hamil-

tonian economics—to a credit system, and to wipe out the casino economy, get rid of the derivatives bubble, and go to national banking, have credit generation of sovereign governments, and then, have an international credit system by linking these different credit systems through clearing houses, so you can have long-term investment in great projects as a remedy to all of these problems.

In 2003 we were in Turkey—we had been invited by the then Prime Minister, Turgut Özal—and my husband made speeches in Istanbul and Ankara, in which he said we need a concert of nations to go back to the sound criteria of the Bretton Woods system. Later he further specified that the only combination of countries which has the power to undo the British Imperial financial system based on the City of London and Wall Street, would be a four power combination of the United States, Russia, China, and India.

This new petition, which calls on the leaders of

EIRNS/Rolf Pauls

Lyndon LaRouche and Turkish Prime Minister Turgut Özal, Ankara, Turkey, July 29, 1987.

these four countries, not to be exclusive, but to have these four countries function as the core group of nations which would form a New Bretton Woods system and then invite others, and all countries who would like to associate with it, would be welcome to join.

Now, this is urgent. As I said, there are many people who say the next financial storm will hit well before the midterm elections. There are many analysts who say the Federal Reserve "tapering," the so-called increase of interest rates, must urgently stop because it is about to blow out the debt bubble.

The Institute of International Finance in Washington has just published a report showing that the total indebtedness of the world is now $247.2 trillion, representing an increase of 11.1% just for the last year. We are sitting on a complete powder keg, and anything could trigger a collapse of the bubble, which if not remedied would then be the trigger of economic chaos with unforeseeable consequences.

We are calling on you, our audience and many other audiences around the world: study this petition. If you agree with it in principle, that we need an urgent change in the monetary system, that we need to go back to a credit system and real economy, and that a powerful combination of countries is necessary to implement it, then sign and circulate it as widely as you can. We want to translate this petition into as many languages as we can—and if you have language skills, help us translate, it because we want a worldwide mobilization of every country, every force, every person on the planet, to appeal to those four leaders—President Trump, President Putin, President Xi Jinping, and Prime Minister Modi—to take this action; and to increase the pressure by putting this on the agenda of the UN General Assembly which starts in September.

Monetarism and a Credit System Compared

Schlanger: Helga, for those who are not familiar with this, your husband, and you also, have emphasized repeatedly that the difference is between a financial system based on monetarism, as opposed to one which is based on credit for physical economy. If you could just summarize that, so people get a sense of why one tends towards bubbles and crashes, and the other, that we're seeing now, for example, with China's Belt and Road Initiative, is the basis for constant growth.

Left, demolition of an abandoned blast furnace, McKeesport, Pa., 2006. Below, homelessness in the U.S. capital, December 2010.

EIRNS/Stuart Lewis

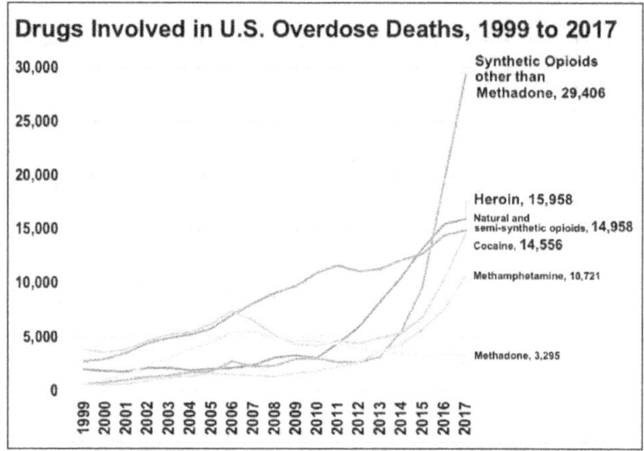

Zepp-LaRouche: My husband recognized that when Nixon decoupled the dollar from FDR's gold reserve system, and got rid of the fixed-exchange rates, this was the first major step in the direction of the deregulation of the financial markets. This was then escalated—Glass-Steagall had been undermined, when Alan Greenspan became the head of the Federal Reserve. When Glass-Steagall was officially repealed in 1999, this was the real starting point for complete deregulation of the financial markets. Many countries implemented legislation which benefitted the speculators at the expense of the physical economy and to the detriment the common good of the people.

Deregulation led to the big crisis in 2008. And there was, for several weeks, a complete shock. I remember very well, many people, even Nicolas Sarkozy, the French President at that time, thought that this was "it," that the system would just collapse. That shock unfortunately didn't last very long, because already at the next G-20 meeting in Washington, in November, they decided to fix it, to use quantitative easing, to use what were eventually zero interest rates, just pumping money into the system to prolong the system which benefits the speculators and at the expense of the common good of the people: destruction of education and culture, cuts in social and medical services, cheap labor, and ruining the economies in their substance.

Since there was nothing done after 2008 to get rid of the root causes of the systemic crisis of 2008, we are now, 10 years later, in a system that is much more indebted, about 40% or more, more indebted than it was in 2008. We now have a bubble which is about to detonate. There has been a lot of looting, a lot of austerity, a lot of low wages, and increases in unemployment.

Contrast that with what China has been doing with the Chinese model of economy, where they uplifted 800 million people in the last 40 years out of poverty; they have created a large, growing middle class, a growing domestic market; they have launched the Belt and Road Initiative, the New Silk Road, bringing economic development to many countries in Eurasia, in Africa, in Latin America. This is just a completely different approach. Just recently China has moved very forcefully to forbid speculation, to forbid Chinese investors from engaging in speculation abroad. There are many countries aware of the weakness of the financial system in the West, and they're preparing to protect themselves against it.

So we are sitting on a powder keg. For example, because of the unfortunate war of sanctions the United States has imposed on many countries, these countries are not sitting idly by, but they are starting to dump U.S. Treasury bonds. This is an amazing thing: It's not just Russia and Turkey, which have started to go out of U.S. Treasuries—Japan also. Japan got rid of, I think $83 billion worth of U.S. Treasuries in the last year. China has started to do it; they have $1.013 trillion in U.S. Treasuries—if they would start dumping those wholesale, it would probably blow out the system right there.

Several countries have started to go out of the dollar for international trade, in favor of denominating their trade in the national currencies involved. All these actions constitute the beginning of the formation of a new economic system which is designed to safeguard against the danger of a blowout.

There is no time to lose. President Trump has spoken very favorably of the American System of economy. He's mentioned Alexander Hamilton, Henry C. Carey, and Abraham Lincoln. What people don't know is that the American System of economy as it was developed by Hamilton, is actually very similar in principle to the Chinese economic model. Most people have no inkling that that's the case, but it's a matter of fact. The same idea drives both systems: that the state has the power and the right to issue credit for investments in the physical economy, provided these investments are based on sound scientific principles, meaning that they have to lead to an increase in productivity and an *increase in the capacity of labor power, to accompany these increases in productivity.*

As long as these principles are safeguarded, there is no reason to think that credit generation by government is inflationary. To the contrary, credit in this fashion has a deflationary effect because it creates new levels of technology. So, that is what is very urgent to understand, and to act on now. We need the right kind of international reform, based on the principles we have been discussing here, to prevent a blow-out and a near-term descent into chaos.

The Wages of Monetarist Sin: Death, as Italian Bridge Collapses

Schlanger: One of the points you made earlier is that with the post-Bretton Woods system, there was a big push for deregulation, also, the so-called "free trade" agreements. Another aspect was privatization, and this plays into the situation in Italy. There's a lot of finger-pointing going on. Except for the policies of the European Union and privatization, it does appear that this Genoa bridge collapse—the Morandi bridge—was completely avoidable.

Zepp-LaRouche: It's not just the European Union. In most European nations, it used to be that, infrastructure belonged to, and was the responsibility of the state. That is actually as it should be, because basic infrastructure does not bring an immediate profit. Infrastructure creates the preconditions for industry, for agriculture, for trade to function. Therefore, when the economy went well, it was always the obligation of the state to take care of it and invest in it.

Now, that was the case in Italy until 1992, when there was a very infamous meeting on Queen Elizabeth's yacht, the *Britannia* [off the coast of Italy], which was actually a conspiratorial meeting of many of the money bags and financial bigwigs. They decided

CC/Salvatore Fabbrizio

View from Coronata of the privatized Morandi motorway bridge in Genoa, Italy, after its partial collapse on Aug. 14, 2018.

not only to go for a huge privatization of all kinds of things—of state-owned industries, of infrastructure, of many things which previously were part of the official public works. And they started to speculate. They speculated the lira down by 30%, and then had foreign investors buy up these things very cheaply. This was a real conspiracy.

Mario Draghi was one of the people involved. He later became a leading banker at Goldman Sachs and now heads the European Central Bank. He has many times ordered huge austerity programs onto Italy, which is one of the reasons why you have the present government in Italy consisting of a coalition of the Lega Nord and the Five Star Movement, both of which are totally euro-critics, because they have seen what the EU austerity policy has done to the Italian economy.

It is the combination of privatization of things which should be public, and massive austerity which has inevitably led to non-investment in infrastructure repair.

Infrastructure has only a certain lifespan. Depending on what categories you are dealing with, infrastructure needs to be repaired after 40 or 50 years, or even 20 years, or 80 years. But in the case of this bridge, which was privatized; it belongs to a larger auto-way called Autostrade, owned by the Benetton family.

Now it turns out that the inspectors, the people who were inspecting the condition of the bridge, had noted that the bridge was in urgent need of repair. Rather than starting repairs immediately, the owners of this private infrastructure decided to postpone the beginning of the repair until September, when the main holiday traffic—the big profit period—would be over, because this is a toll system. This bridge goes toward the port of Genoa and then all the islands, and also to France. So a lot of tourists and people who go to the beaches travel in the summer over this bridge. Obviously, this looting of big profits was the reason why the repair was postponed.

This is all now under investigation, and there is a big move for the Italian government to renationalize this infrastructure, which is causing a huge freak-out on the side of the privatizers. I think this is a very interesting development, which is not only affecting Italy. Now there is a big debate going on about the condition of bridges and other infrastructure in Germany. It turns out that 12% of all bridges in Germany are regarded as highly unsafe, and the same thing that happened in Italy could happen in Germany at any moment.

The infrastructure in the United States is in an absolutely abysmal condition. I think that this is really a reflection of the policies that started in 1971 with the abandoning, the destruction of the Bretton Woods system through Nixon. We need an urgent reversal of this policy; this is why this petition is circulating.

Turn Russiagate into Muellergate

Schlanger: I want to take up next an aspect of the continuing unfolding of the Russiagate story. This week, President Trump lifted the security clearance of [Obama's former CIA Director] John Brennan. This was, in our opinion, long overdue, but it caused an enormous panic in the media. Brennan wrote an op-ed in the *New York Times*, asserting that Trump colluded—again without presenting any evidence. Also, [FBI agent] Peter Strzok was fired. We're talking about a 90-day perspective for the economy and the security side of this—ending Russiagate. Where do things stand on that, Helga?

Zepp-LaRouche: President Trump's lawyer Rudy Giuliani said that it's high time that Brennan is put in front of a grand jury investigation. Giuliani said that Special Counsel Robert Mueller should wrap up his

It's right because he is irresponsible and untrustworthy and has politicized intelligence.

Russia probe and submit his report by September 7, or his investigation should be shut down, because otherwise it would constitute an interference in the November midterm elections. Several Congressional committees are working—despite the summer break—interviewing people under subpoena. Everything centers on the role of the British colluding with the Obama intelligence apparatus in creating this coup attempt against President Trump. The reason we are in a 90-day countdown, so to speak, is that there is right now this investigation, pointing to the intervention and interference of the British government, the MI6, the GCHQ (the equivalent of the NSA), of the British secret services, into the U.S. election.

This is the biggest scandal in the history of the United States. Were these Congressional investigations to be shut down, I think the United States would probably never recover from it. It's very clear from the hysteria of the Dem-

ocrats and some neo-cons in the Republican Party, but especially also the so-called mainstream media, that they are completely freaked out because they all were part of this collusion.

In Nazi Germany, the word *gleichgeschaltet* [synchronized] was used to characterize the unified line of the media under Reich Minister of Propaganda Joseph Goebbels. Now take a look at the behavior of the U.S. media. On Aug. 16—in a modern-day example of *Gleichschaltung—three hundred newspapers* ran editorials in an absolutely incredible attack against Trump. Does anyone think that isn't a conspiracy? Three hundred papers coordinating their action. Call it a conspiracy, or a plan, whatever you want to call it, but these so-called "mainstream" newspapers, bawling about freedom of the press, are the same media that are covering up the biggest scandal in the history of the United States, trying to give it a spin, so that ordinary people won't be able to penetrate it.

Therefore, it is extremely urgent that Congress acts and that the American public acts to back up Trump to declassify all of the documents having to do with Christopher Steele, and having to do with the FISA [Foreign Intelligence Surveillance Act] Court warrants. *All of these things must be declassified!*

There is a new article out by the expert on this matter—Barbara Boyd—with the title "Fish Stinks from the Head Down," an update on the latest inconsistencies in the stories of Peter Strzok, Lisa Page, and all of these people participating in the coup attempt against Trump. Get this article. Go the LaRouche PAC website, download it and read it [https://larouchepac.com/20180810/fish-stinks-head-down-update-mueller-inquisition]. Then circulate it as widely as possible, because that is the very best thing you can do: The truth is coming out, and we are getting this into the hands of those who need to understand what is really going on in this unbelievable story.

Schlanger: There are some other very important developments, starting with Russia. Prime Minister Dmitry Medvedev is denouncing the new U.S. sanctions against Russia as an act of economic warfare. What do you have to say about that?

Sanctions Don't Stop Putin's Humanity

Zepp-LaRouche: Obviously the imposition of new sanctions on Russia is an effort by bipartisan forces in the Senate to take away the power of the President to define foreign policy. After Trump met with Putin in Helsinki, the hysteria completely went into overdrive, in an effort by the Senate to continue what it started last summer with the so-called CAATSA [the Countering America's Adversaries Through Sanctions Act], by imposing what Lindsey Graham called "sanctions from Hell." These "sanctions from Hell," if they were all implemented by November, would basically ban Russian banks from international work; would ban trading in Russian bonds; and would therefore completely cripple the Russian economy, at least under the present circumstances. That's why Prime Minister Medvedev called these sanctions a declaration of economic war, and vowed that Russia will absolutely take decisive countermeasures.

We have already seen part of Russia's countermeasures when Foreign Minister Lavrov was in Ankara, Turkey discussing with President Erdogan and others, a shift away from the dollar into trade in the national currencies. If this thing escalates, if the trade war with China escalates, with sanctions on all kinds of countries, it could build to an uncontrollable situation. Therefore, we have been insisting that the Muellergate operation against Trump must be shut down immediately. Trump's natural impulse is to seek a better relationship with Russia. And he was doing very well with Xi Jinping before. I think that under the urgency of the situation, the making of a Four-Power Agreement, which then would be supported by many other nations in the world, is an absolutely urgent but also realistic possibility. It must happen now.

Schlanger: And again, people should go to the

Russian Prime Minister Dimitri Medvedev.

Schiller Institute website and get the new petition that calls for an emergency summit for a Four-Power meeting to enact a New Bretton Woods.

Helga, two things on the positive side, one of which is actually quite delightful. You have the South Korea-North Korea talks coming up, President Moon meeting with Chairman Kim. Then also, President Putin being invited back to Austria under interesting circumstances. What do you think?

Zepp-LaRouche: President Moon Jae-in of South Korea has launched a very interesting initiative preparatory to his going to Pyongyang in about a month. He has proposed a Northeast Asia Economic Railway Initiative, whereby the railway systems of South and North Korea, Russia, and China are to be integrated and be the basis of a major economic program. I think this is a very good thing, and despite the media—who basically pooh-pooh the Trump-Kim Summit all the time—all the parties are saying it *is* working, from the Trump administration, from Russia, from South Korea, and from China. They all say it is absolutely proceeding, as it was discussed between Trump and Kim Jong-un in Singapore, and it actually is progressing in a good way. So, this is a very good development.

The last thing you mentioned I find quite amusing, because Putin, on his way to Germany, where he will meet with Chancellor Angela Merkel tomorrow, will be attending the wedding of Austrian Foreign Minister Karin Kneissl. When she invited him a couple of months ago in Vienna, he said, "Yes I will come," and now he'll be there. In the face of all the anti-Russian hysteria, the fact that the Austrian Foreign Minister would invite Putin to her wedding is actually quite a human response; it should be normal, it should make people happy.

But in these times of Marco Rubio going haywire and Sen. Lindsey Graham and many other people being in a worse-than-McCarthy fit, it does create a flutter. But hopefully such simply human interaction as shown by Putin will occur often in the future when we have a New Paradigm. I think everyone should just enjoy it.

Sign and Circulate the Petition

Schlanger: Absolutely! Helga, is there anything else you want to cover?

Zepp-LaRouche: No, I just would really like people to look at this petition. It has the potential to move the relevant heads of state if enough people in enough countries sign it. We want to change the agenda. Right now, the only way you can address all of these many problems—the refugee crisis, the lack of credit for rebuilding the economy. If people have questions, if you don't understand why this is the solution, the pre-step for all solutions, contact us, get in a discussion with us, send us an email. Raise the level of political discussion around you to a higher level. If you just try to solve each little problem within its little setting, you cannot do it.

Einstein once said, do not think that you can solve a major problem with the same methods which were the reason for it to exist in the first place. You need a different method. What we are here proposing is a different method: to operate at a higher level of reason, of strategic cooperation. I do not think it's impossible because you already have the emergence of a new economic system anyway. The BRICS, the New Silk Road, the Shanghai Cooperation Organization, the Eurasian Economic Union; there are already many processes in the direction of a new economic-financial architecture. But to actually bring that new economic-financial architecture into being requires thinking on a strategic level.

So, please sign and circulate this petition. Get as many signatures as you are able.

Schlanger: Well, thank you very much, Helga. We'll see you next week.

Zepp-LaRouche: Yes, hopefully next week.

NEW RELEASE, **Volume II**

The New Silk Road Becomes the World Land-Bridge:

A Shared Future For Humanity

The spirit of the New Silk Road is changing the world for the better. The exciting overview in this new 440-page Volume II report updates the roadmap given in Volume I, on the coming into being of the World Land-Bridge for development and peace. BRICS countries have a strategy to prevent war and economic catastrophe. It's time for the rest of the world to join!

Includes:
Introduction by Helga Zepp-LaRouche, "A Shared Future for Humanity."

Progress Reports on development corridors worldwide, spurred by China's Belt and Road Initiative. Features 140 maps.

Principles of Physical Economy by Lyndon LaRouche, especially his "Four Laws" for emergency action in the Trans-Atlantic.

Soft cover (440 pages)
Domestic Price: $60. Shipping cost included in price.
Foreign Price: $60. Add $15 per copy for shipping.
Order from **newparadigm.schillerinstitute.com**
Tel 1 703 297 8368

America-China Relations: The Longer View

by William Jones

The impetus for this article was a lecture given by the author at Zhejiang University on May 19, as the keynote of a two-day forum on U.S.-China relations and the Trump Administration.

During the 234 years that the United States has had relations with China, that relationship has largely been amicable and mutually beneficial. The origins of both nations have played a role in this. Until the American Revolution, the English and other settlers in North America had been under the thumb of the British Empire. China, while never a colony of any nation, would also feel the oppressive heel of the British Empire from the outbreak of the first Opium War in 1839. Both cultures, in different ways, have been affected by that experience. And the good-will shown by Americans toward China during its more difficult periods has been based on a genuine aversion of Americans to having any country under an oppressor's heel.

This has to do with the unique history of the United States, the creation of which was the end result of so many failed attempts to change the oligarchical system predominant in Europe. The migration to the new colonies in America included some of the best elements from European society, and particularly from the British Isles, who had found it impossible to change, or to live with, the oligarchical system that was 17th Century Britain.

The lack of any fixed social structure in the colonies gave much more leeway for them to attempt to fashion their own institutions of government in a way that

The Empress of China *leaving New York harbor, the first U.S. trading ship to sail to the Far East, February 22, 1784.*

would reflect the notion of the equality of man, which had been brutally suppressed under the European regimes. It was the refusal of the British oligarchy to allow anything like that to happen that led to the outbreak of the American Revolution, whose effects reverberated around the world.

Particularly during the first century of America's sovereign existence, this cultural heritage imbued the inhabitants of this new Republic with a repugnance toward oligarchies and hereditary nobilities, and it inspired them with a preference for a system based on merit and achievement rather than on blood relationship.

George Washington's keen desire to quickly build a university in the new capital city of the United States was aimed at preventing American youth from having to go abroad to study in Europe and perhaps adopting there, the old aristocratic modes of thought.

It is true that the United States has at times forgotten those important lessons of our history—or completely ignored them. During the first part of the last century, and during the Cold War and McCarthy era, the United States often took on the role of oppressor itself. And the continual wars of the last few decades, from Vietnam to Iraq, bear witness to the loss of that republican spirit. This betrayal—or at best ignoring—of our revolutionary heritage was not, however, "made in America," but instead was the result of the decades-long successful effort—particularly after the death of Franklin Roosevelt—to woo America into a "Special Relationship" with our historic enemy, the United Kingdom, and to import the geopolitical designs of that Empire into American foreign policy.

It is with the hope of reviving the real history of America that I have attempted to illuminate the periods of U.S.-China cooperation which truly reflect the American spirit, as opposed to that phony narrative of the Anglo-American "special relationship."

The New Republic Sets Sail

On February 22, 1784, a three-masted, square-rigged sailing ship of 360 tons, *The Empress of China*, left New York harbor carrying a full load of goods, including 30 tons of ginseng, on a six-month voyage to Canton (Guangzhou), China. This was the first U.S. trading ship to set out on a voyage to the Far East. Prior to the American Revolution, Americans could only trade in British bottoms and under the British flag. And Great Britain virtually ruled the waves. With independence, trade with Europe for an independent American vessel was virtually excluded by this British monopoly, and the British were brooking no competitors—particularly from a nation which had broken from "the Empire." So, the voyage was also the

Maj. Samuel Shaw

first major assertion at sea of America's sovereignty.

The significance of the mission was ever-present in the minds of the voyagers. The ship's captain, John Green, had run smuggling missions and raids against the British fleet during the Revolution. He was released from the Continental Navy to take command of this particular vessel. Samuel Shaw, the supercargo (manager of the ship's cargo), had been a major in the American Revolution and had served as an aide-de-camp to General Henry Knox. Shaw had also fought at Trenton, Monmouth and Yorktown, where Lafayette praised the work of Shaw's artillery. A testimonial by George Washington said of Shaw that he "distinguished himself in everything which could entitle him to the character of an intelligent, active and brave officer."

Painting by Robert Edge Pine

Robert Morris

Both Green and Shaw were members of the Society of the Cincinnati, as were five other crew members. Shaw was a founding member of the Society and, according to Timothy Pickering, had written its constitution. The ship itself had also served as a privateer during the Revolution.

The ship's crew carried with it a copy of the *Declaration of Independence*, as was common in American ships of the time, proud to show foreigners this remarkable founding document. The ship also carried official treaties and an official letter from the President and the Secretary of Congress (the country was still operating under the Articles of Confederation), addressed to any foreign rulers they might encounter during their voyage.

The chief financier of the voyage was Robert Morris, a signer of the Declaration of Independence, and the chief financier of the American Revolution. Writing to John Jay, who was serving as foreign minister, Morris said of the voyage, "I am sending some ships to China in order to encourage others in the adventurous pursuit of Commerce, and I wish to see a foundation laid for an American Navy." As the ship sailed out of New York harbor, symbolically on George Washington's birthday, she fired off a thirteen-gun salute, which was responded to by the cannons of the fort on shore. (This was the highest salute at the time, symbolizing the thirteen states of the Union.) The sailing of the *Empress* set the stage for other ships to engage in trade with the Far East.

Shaw would write an extensive report on the trip to John Jay. While he dutifully reported on the conditions of trade with the Chinese, he also kept Jay fully abreast of the various activities of the British in the region and the growing conflict between the British and the other European traders. He also noted the total British disdain shown for the American presence there. Shaw would later be named U.S. Consul to China, and Thomas Randall, who was also on the maiden voyage of the *Empress* to China, would be made Vice-Consul, keeping Treasury Secretary Alexander Hamilton well-informed of the trade activities of the other nations in Asia-Pacific region.

The American Confucius

The voyage of the *Empress of China* was not the first encounter of the new American Republic with China. Our own philosopher and scientist Benjamin Franklin had already made acquaintance with China through his travels in Europe, where he served as minister to France during the Revolution, and his own readings of the works of Confucius, that were becoming available to the West at the time.

Franklin's European sojourn coincided with the increasing interest in what was considered the exotic Far East engendered by the extensive reports coming from the Jesuit missionaries who were serving in China as advisors to the Qing Emperor. The Jesuit mis-

Painting by Joseph Siffred Duplessis

Benjamin Franklin was greatly influenced by Confucius (left), as reflected in his writings on morality.

Anonymous Qing Dynasty Court Painter

The great Kangxi Emperor.

sions, while focused initially on conversions, were also an opportunity for Chinese scholars to make their first acquaintance with developments in Western science since the Renaissance. And the inquisitiveness of the Chinese, particularly that of the great Emperor Kangxi, regarding these new sciences, led him to allow Jesuit astronomers to serve on the Imperial Board of Astronomy in Beijing. The letters the Jesuits wrote back to Europe gave the Europeans their first real, detailed picture of this Empire in the East.

In Philadelphia, Franklin read much of the Chinese material which was arriving from Europe based on the missionaries' reports. In 1738, Franklin was already studying Father Jean-Baptiste Du Halde's *Description of the Empire of China*. In 1767, Franklin published in his own *Pennsylvania Gazette* a series of articles entitled, "The Morals of Confucius." This was taken directly from an English translation of a book published in Latin, *Confucius Sinarum Philosophus*, by the Belgian missionary,

Philippe Couplet, a correspondent of Gottfried Leibniz, which summarized the thoughts of Confucius. And Franklin's Quaker friend in Philadelphia, James Logan, had one of the largest collection of works at the time about China, primarily from the Jesuit collections.

A more comprehensive work on China, *Memoires concernant l'histoire, les sciences, les arts, les moeurs, les usages, &c. des Chinois*, was published in 1776 in seventeen volumes on the basis of the Jesuit letters. The first fifteen volumes of this collection were found in Franklin's personal library and are now housed at the Princeton University Library.

In his own works, Franklin made numerous comments on the virtues of the Chinese. He was greatly influenced by the works of Confucius, and indeed, much of his personal writings on morality reflect this Confucian influence. He also expressed an interest in traveling to China, and, during his own travels to Europe, he would often interrogate sailors he met who had been to China and to the Far East. The series on Confucius in the *Pennsylvania Gazette*, underlined three important concerns of Confucius' philosophy, to which Franklin in his own life and writings also adhered:

1. Of what we ought to do to cultivate our Minds, and regulate our Manner.
2. Of the Method by which it is necessary to instruct and guide others.
3. Of the Care every one ought to have to tend to the Sovereign Good, to adhere thereunto, and, I may say repose himself therein.

Confucius' moral philosophy, Franklin wrote, was "the gate through which it is necessary to pass to arrive at the sublimest wisdom and most perfect." Franklin also had a high regard for the principles of governance in China, hoping that some of these might be implemented in the new Republic. He promoted the idea of using the Chinese system of regular censuses of the population and regular statistics on pro-

The Pennsylvania Gazette, in which Franklin published some of the moral philosophy of Confucius.

duction. Franklin was also opposed to any system of aristocracy in the United States and agreed with the Chinese views that "honors" must ascend from below, based on a person's merits and not be descended hereditarily (from father to son). Franklin lauded the Chinese system of meritocracy, which brought to the top those who showed their capabilities, rather than their patrimony.

In a letter to George Wakefield dated July 6, 1749, Franklin wrote: "When he [Confucius] saw his country sunk in vice, and wickedness of all kinds triumphant, he applied himself first to the grandees; and having by his doctrine won them to the cause of virtue, the commons followed in multitudes. The mode has a wonderful influence on mankind."

Franklin also wished to follow the Chinese in cultivating silk production and in utilizing their navigation technology. The Chinese were the first to tightly caulk compartments of their ships, so that if one were breached, the others would not be filled with water and the ship could be saved. Franklin discovered in England the soybean that was grown in China, and he sent some soybeans to his friend, John Bartram, the noted botanist, to study for possible cultivation in North America. Franklin was also in favor of the United States sending an envoy to China, feeling that one sent from this new nation, uncluttered by a colonial past, would not raise the same concerns as those raised by European envoys, who had their own clear geopolitical goals in their relationship with China.

U.S. Struggle with Britain in the Pacific

The War of 1812 placed U.S. and British ships in conflict in the Pacific as well as the Atlantic, with growing British interest in controlling the Hawaiian Islands as a dagger pointed at the heart of North America.

After the war, the United States sent the first warship, *Ontario*, around Cape Horn to assert an American title to the lower Columbia Valley on the Pacific coast, which was also claimed as an area of interest by Great Britain and by Russia, which had already established

British gunboat diplomacy forces China to cede territory and accept opium importation.

Library of Congress

itself in Alaska and along the western coast of the American continent.

Although U.S. trade with the Far East did develop through the first half of the 19th Century, it remained far below that of the Europeans, particularly that of the British, who would remain the dominant players in Japan and China for many years and were doing everything possible to hinder American products and influence in the region.

When the British launched the First Opium War in 1839, America remained outside the fray and, ignoring British calls for a trade boycott, continued to trade with China. Even though a small number of U.S. merchants were recruited into the opium trade, American policy remained officially one of friendship with China.

The U.S. government sent two ships under Commodore Lawrence Kearny to China, which arrived in early 1842. The first thing that Kearny did when he arrived in Canton, was to announce that his government would not sanction any opium smuggling under the American flag, and American merchants were warned that they faced serious risks if they did so. To make his point, Kearny even forced an American schooner, the *Ariel*, to dispose of its illegal cargo, and deprived her of her American papers. China's

Commodore Lawrence Kearny

Viceroy of Canton would later hail this friendly act and go on to declare that American ships had always obeyed the law.

The First Opium War led to the first of the "unequal treaties." The Treaty of Nanking in 1842 stipulated that China should pay the British an indemnity, cede the territory of Hong Kong, open five new ports to British trade, and establish a "fair and reasonable" tariff.

When the victorious British succeeded in wringing another oppressive treaty from the Chinese, the Supplementary Treaty of the Bogue, the United States felt that it also should ensure its interest by a formal commercial agreement under these new conditions. The ensuing Treaty of Wanghia in 1844 gave the United States all the privileges won by the British based on most-favored-nation status, and also reasserted the principle of extraterritoriality, meaning that Americans who were accused of a crime would be tried under American rather than Chinese law.

But the treaty reasserted the U.S. prohibition of the opium trade, and waived extraterritoriality for Americans who trafficked in opium. They would be subject to the full severity of Chinese law. The treaty allowed the construction of American schools, hospitals and churches in the treaty ports, which encouraged the work of the American Protestant churches. It also made it lawful for U.S. citizens to employ Chinese scholars to teach any of the languages of the Empire, or to assist in writing and research, which had previously been restricted by the Qing authorities. Later in the century, the work of the Protestant missionaries would serve as the basis of the development of a modern educational system in China.

The treaty contained an important clause, saying that in any conflict between China and any third power, where any other nation acted "unjustly or oppressively," the United States would "exert their good offices" to settle the question amicably. This gave the United States a special role in the diplomatic community in China.

In the Second Opium War, 1856-1860, the British captured Canton and moved on to Tianjin, a port close to the Chinese capital. The Chinese were forced to agree to new terms in the Treaty of Tianjin, in which several new ports were opened to foreign trade. In addition, foreigners were allowed to travel up to 600 miles along the Yangtze, and foreign missionaries were allowed freedom of movement throughout the country. In a separate agreement signed in Shanghai, Britain's despicable opium trade was given full legal status.

When the Chinese later balked at ratifying the oppressive treaty, the British and French returned to Tianjin, attacked the capital, Peking, and deliberately destroyed the cultural treasure of the Yuanming Garden, the elaborate summer palace of the Emperor. The devastated garden remains so even today, as a constant reminder to the Chinese public of the days when China was under the thumb of European powers. Because

Anson Burlingame

of this new military action, the Chinese were forced to sign the Beijing Convention, in which they agreed to ratify the treaty of Tianjin, and in addition, were forced to cede Hong Kong and Kowloon to the British.

China and the Lincoln Presidency

Abraham Lincoln had far more immediate, more deadly problems than relations with China when he took office in 1861. Nevertheless, the thinly veiled British and French support for the Confederacy made it necessary for Lincoln to secure the country on the foreign policy front—in particular, to prevent other nations from giving any support to the rebellion. His choice of envoys to the various European powers was therefore of great importance.

His choice for envoy to the Austro-Hungarian Empire was Anson Burlingame, a former Republican congressman from Massachusetts. Burlingame traveled to Paris on his way to the Austro-Hungarian capital with Lincoln's appointment papers, where he suddenly received word that the Austro-Hungarian Emperor was not prepared to accept him as the United States representative. Burlingame had been one of the major hosts of Hungarian freedom fighter Louis Kossuth during his visit to the United States in 1852, which made him *persona non grata* at the Austrian court. As a result, he was reassigned to the relatively inferior post of U.S. envoy (Minister) to the Chinese Empire, a sudden twist of fate which would prove to be of great benefit to China and to U.S.- China relations.

Burlingame, who had not previously been involved in Far Eastern

Cartoon from Le Petit Journal
Britain, Germany, Russia, France and Japan carving up the China. 1898.

policy, devoted himself to a crash course in it. One of his teachers when he arrived in Beijing, was S. Wells Williams, an eminent American Presbyterian missionary and sinologist, who was serving as the secretary of the American legation. Also, Lincoln's Secretary of State, William Seward, was fortunately one of the first secretaries to take a keen interest in the Far East, and he gave Burlingame the support he needed.

At the same time, through greater contact with Western envoys, who were now allowed by treaty in the capital, the Chinese Government had realized that it needed to set up

Prince Gong

something akin to a Foreign Office. So, in 1861, the Empire established the Tsungli Yamen (Office for General Management), which was supervised by a controlling board of five officials, the most important being Prince Gong, the uncle of the under-aged Emperor Tongzhi.

Burlingame quickly became the most important foreign envoy in Beijing. The fact that an American soldier of fortune, Frederick Ward, was also leading Chinese government forces against the Taiping rebels, created a positive image of the United States in Chinese eyes. Concerned that foreign merchants were lobbying to "divide the spoils" after the Anglo-French intervention in 1860, Burlingame pulled together the other envoys around a cooperative policy, in which they issued a document that reaffirmed their treaty prerogatives to trade and live in the prescribed ports, but also stated that they would not threaten the territorial integrity of China or the jurisdiction of the Chinese government—nor would they intervene in Chinese internal affairs, except to uphold the rights accorded them by treaty.

This agreement resulted in measures by the Chinese government to further facilitate trade with the foreign powers. Burlingame's initiatives also won him the support and trust of Prince Gong.

Burlingame was convinced that China should develop its natural resources. He persuaded Prince Gong to bring the American geologist, Raphael Pumpelly, to do a survey of coal resources in China. He further persuaded the Prince to sponsor a Chinese translation of Henry Wheaton's *Elements of International Law,* to acquaint Chinese officials with that important subject. Burlingame also encouraged the construction of railroads in China, which were frowned upon by the Chinese government because it feared giving foreign companies too much influence over Chinese transportation. Burlingame pressed the State Department for a larger legation in Peking and for salaried consuls in the principal ports. While unable to eliminate extraterritoriality entirely, Burlingame allowed Chinese citizens to give evidence in cases which came under the purview of the U.S. Minister, something that had not been allowed previously.

With the Civil War raging in the United States, there was also a clear danger that rebel privateers would try to use Chinese ports for refurbishing and gathering supplies, or even commandeering new vessels to prey on American ships. Burlingame succeeded in getting the Tsungli Yamen to give orders to refuse all succor to Confederate warships prowling in the East Indies.

Prince Gong would often consult with Burlingame on foreign affairs. In 1867, when he learned that Burlingame was preparing to relinquish his post and return to the United States, he expressed great concern. Burlingame tried to console him by saying that he would continue to do his best to garner support for China in the United States.

Before his departure, however, Prince Gong asked Burlingame to give up his post as U.S. envoy, to serve as an envoy of China at the head of a delegation he was preparing to send to the European capitals and to the United States. This was a measure that Burlingame and others had earlier urged on him to create greater understanding of China in the Western capitals.

At first, Burlingame thought he was joking, but he soon realized that the offer was real. The great trust he had acquired during his stay had assured the Chinese that he would truly represent their interests. And while

Anson Burlingame (center) led the first Chinese foreign mission in 1868.

they would also be sending some of their own top diplomats, it was felt that Burlingame's knowledge of the Western capitals would ensure the success of the delegation. Burlingame agreed, and on November 21, 1867, he resigned his official commission in American service and entered the service of the Emperor of China as a "high minister extraordinary and plenipotentiary."

The first stop was the United States. Beginning with its landing in San Francisco, the delegation was widely celebrated. Despite growing uneasiness among some Californians about the large Chinese immigration there, all were elated by the possibility of greater trade with China. The delegation then sailed via Panama to New York and Washington, where they met with President Andrew Johnson at the White House. During the interim, Secretary of State Seward had drawn up a treaty based on many of the recommendations he and Burlingame had worked out regarding China. The delegation signed the treaty in Washington, subject, of course, to ratification by the higher authorities in Beijing.

Speaking at a banquet in New York on June 23, 1868, attended by many of the leading lights of the day, including FDR's grandfather Warren Delano and

First group of 30 Chinese boys sent to study in the U.S. in 1872.

Townsend Harris, the U.S. envoy to Japan, Burlingame gave a moving defense of China's position.

She comes with your own international laws; she tells you that she is willing to come into relations according to it, that she is willing to abide by its provisions, that she is willing to take its obligations for its privileges. [Cheers] She asks you to forget your ancient prejudices, to abandon your assumptions of superiority, and to submit your questions with her, as she proposes to submit her questions with you to the arbitrament of reason. [Cheers]

Speaking in Boston, at an August 21 banquet in honor of the Chinese delegation, Burlingame explained the fundamental significance of the new treaty:

I say China has been put upon terms of equality. Her subjects have been put upon a footing of those of the most favored nations, so that now the Chinese stands with the Briton or the Frenchman, the Russian, the Prussian and everybody else. And not only so, but by a Consulary clause in that treaty they are given a diplomatic status by which those privileges can be defended. That treaty also strikes down all disabilities on account of religious faith. It recalls the great doctrine of the Constitution which gives to a man the right to hold any faith which his conscience may dictate to him. Under that treaty the Chinese may spread their marble altars to the blue vault of heaven and may worship the spirit which dwells beyond. That treaty opens the gleaming gates of our public institutions to the students of China. That treaty strikes down or reprobates—

that is the word—the infamous Coolie trade. It sustains the law of 1862, drafted by Mr. Elliot of Massachusetts, and pledges the nation forever to hold that trade criminal … It invites free immigration into the country of those sober and industrious people by whose quiet labor we have been enabled to push the Pacific railroad over the summits of the Sierra Nevada. Woolen mills have been enabled to run because of this labor with profit. And the crops of California, more valuable than all her gold, have been gathered by them. I am glad the United States had the courage to apply her great principles of equality.

Leaving the United States, the delegation would travel to Great Britain, France, Germany and Russia. Burlingame was intent on resolving the remaining border issues between China and Russia. Arriving in St. Petersburg, they met with Czar Alexander II, the liberator of the serfs, who received them warmly. "I am very glad to see you here," he told the delegates, "since your presence is new proof of the peaceful and friendly relations which have always existed between us and China. I hope that your negotiations will only confirm these excellent relations. I am at the same time very glad to see the interests of China represented by a citizen of a friendly state which is especially sympathetic to us." But tragedy struck at this point when Burlingame caught pneumonia and died, a martyr to the cause of this, China's earlier "opening up."

In an obituary of Burlingame, written by his friend, Mark Twain, Twain commented on Burlingame's character,

It is not easy to comprehend, at an instant's warning, the exceeding magnitude of the loss which mankind sustains in this death, the loss which all nations and all peoples sustain in it. For he had outgrown the narrow citizenship of a state and become a citizen of the world; and his charity was large enough and his great heart warm enough to feel for all its races and to labor for them.

Creating Native Cadre for Industrial Take-Off

By the end of the Civil War and the beginning of the construction of the Transcontinental Railroad, which was completed in 1867, it was clear that the United States would become more directly involved in the Pacific trade and in trade with China. Even President Lincoln, in his last Annual Message to Congress in December 1864, referred to this development. He said,

The rebellion which has so long been flagrant in China has at last been suppressed, with the cooperating good offices of this Government and of the other Western commercial States. The judicial consular establishment there has become very difficult and onerous, and it will need legislative revision to adapt it to the extension of our commerce and to the more intimate intercourse which has been instituted with the Government and people of that vast Empire. China seems to be accepting with hearty good will the conventional laws which regulate commercial and social intercourse among the Western nations.

And the final victory over the slave power had profound implications for the rest of humanity, in underlining the universal nature of human freedom. Sun Yat-sen's borrowing from Lincoln's Gettysburg Address for his Three Principles was just one example of that influence.

American interest in the China trade would only increase with time. When Ulysses Grant was elected president in 1868, this interest was at its height. In seven of the eight Annual Messages given by Grant, he referred to the importance of the Pacific region for the United States. Later, when he had left the presidency, he would play an even greater role in his attempts to mediate peace between the two most important Asian powers, China and Japan.

Right from the beginning of his presidency, Grant also made it clear that his administration would be fully supportive of the Burlingame Treaty, which had not been ratified by China when Grant became president. Grant's Secretary of State, Hamilton Fish, wrote in a letter to George Bancroft, the U.S. envoy to Germany: "The great principle which underlies the articles of July 1868 [the Seward-Burlingame Treaty] is the recognition of the sovereign authority of the Imperial government at Peking over their social, commercial, and political relations with the western powers." Fish called the treaty one of "amity," rather than of the "force" which had characterized the previous "unequal treaties."

There were reformers in the Qing court who understood the necessity of bringing China into the modern era, if the country was to withstand the pressure of the more powerful Western nations. One of these reformers was Zeng Guofan. Marquis Zeng had been a commander of the Qing Army in the fight against the Taiping rebels, and in 1860, he was appointed the new imperial commissioner for most of southern China. Zeng was also assisted by Li Hongzhang, who would command the Qing Navy in the fight against the Taiping rebels. In 1863, Zeng brought in Yung Wing, one of the first Chinese students educated in the West, a graduate of Yale University, as his adviser.

The successful activity of Yung Wing also made clear the importance of sending Chinese youth abroad to become educated, particularly in areas of technology and engineering. Yung Wing, with his own connections at Yale, succeeded in setting up a Chinese Educational Mission where Chinese youth could study abroad to attain the vital skills needed for modernization. Zeng Guofan and Li Hongzhang submitted a memorial to the Qing Government calling for such a mission. The choice of the United States was obvious because of the guarantee of the Burlingame Treaty. The memorial received the support of the Qing court, and the first batch of students arrived in Hartford, Connecticut in 1872.

The year 1876 was the occasion of the Centennial of the founding of the United States, and the outgoing Grant Administration had arranged a major international exhibition in Philadelphia with exhibits from most of the countries around the world. Both Japan and China had exhibits. The centerpiece of the Centennial were the exhibits showcasing the major advances the United States had made in science and technology since the end of the Civil War. People came from all over the world to see them.

Li Hongzhang had assigned Li Gui, a translator for the Imperial Maritime Commission, to travel to the United States and Europe, and to attend the Centennial and report back on his observations, which he did in a book introduced by Li Hongzhang. Of course, the Chinese students in Hartford were also at the Centennial. President Grant, who had opened the exhibition, made a return visit towards the end, and held a reception for the Chinese students, shaking hands and speaking briefly with each one. While the China Educational

The Corliss Centennial Engine at the opening ceremonies of the Centennial Exposition in Philadelphia, 1876.

Mission would be terminated all too soon, the students who passed through it would later serve as the most important technical cadre in China's early modernization attempts.

Grant as Mediator in China-Japan Dispute

As Grant was leaving office in 1877, he made arrangements to take a trip around the world with his wife and son. Except as a soldier in the Mexican War, Grant had never traveled abroad. But with his renown as the victorious general of the Civil War and for his two terms as President, he would be received like royalty wherever he went (often to his chagrin).

He traveled to many European capitals, visiting Germany, France, Russia, Spain and Italy, and meeting with Bismarck, Alexander II and Pope Leo XIII. He then traveled to Egypt, to the Middle East and then on to Asia. He spent considerable time in India, and already on his way there, he was appalled by the British treatment of the native populations in the countries of the Middle East, where British control along this strategic "route to India" was almost total. Speaking to one of his traveling companions, John Russell Young, who kept a written record of the trip, Grant said,

As I was traveling through the East, I tried to find something in the policy of the English gov-

U.S. Grant's audience with the Emperor and Empress of Japan, 1877.

ernment to approve. But I could not. I was fresh from England, and wanted to be in accord with men who had shown me as much kindness as Lord Beaconsfield and his colleagues. But it was impossible. England's policy in the East is hard, reactionary, and selfish. No one can visit those wonderful lands on the Mediterranean without seeing what they might be under a good government. As I understand the Eastern Question, the great obstacle to the good government of these countries is England. Unless she can control them herself she will allow no one else. That I call a selfish policy. I cannot see the humanity of keeping those noble countries under a barbarous rule, merely because there are apprehensions about the road to India.

When he arrived in China, Grant held discussions with Prince Gong and with Li Hongzhang. China was then in a dispute with Japan over the Liu-qiu (Ryukyu) Islands. In 1874, Japan had invaded Taiwan, which was considered a Chinese tributary. Now further action by the Japanese on the Liu-qiu islands could be the straw that broke the camel's back, leading Chinese to accuse their government of forfeiting its sovereign rights. In Grant's meetings with Li and with Prince Gong, they requested his assistance in mediating with Japan, knowing the prestige he would have with the Japanese. Grant was eager to help, because he saw that a war between these two countries would open the gate to more aggressive acts by the European powers, particularly the British, who dominated the trade of Asia.

From China, Grant arrived in Japan. Here he was given the unprecedented opportunity of a private discussion with the Meiji Emperor. Speaking with the Emperor, President Grant expressed his disgust with the operations of the European powers in the Far East, which, he said, "made his blood boil." He warned the Emperor, as he had Bismarck earlier, against taking loans from these powers—he might lose his sovereignty in the bargain as Egypt had. Grant stressed the importance of Japanese and Chinese independence and urged the Emperor to try to come to an understanding with China on the Liu-qiu Islands, in order to avoid a conflict which would only benefit the European powers. He also urged the Japanese side, as the militarily stronger power, to show magnanimity, so as to prevent a loss of face by China, which would only cause further enmity.

Grant would also urge the State Department to play a role in helping avoid any conflict between these two powers. Writing to the State Department from Tokyo, Grant reported on his discussions and expressed his clear view of the matter:

> In the vast east embracing more than two thirds of the human population of the world there are but two nations even partially free from the domination and dictation of some one or other of the European powers, with intelligence and strength enough to maintain their independence: Japan and China are the two nations, the people of both are brave, intelligent, frugal and industrious. With a little more advancement in civilization, mechanics, engineering, etc., they could throw off the offensive treaties which now cripple and humiliate them and could enter into competition for the world's commerce. Much more employment for the people would result from the change and vastly more effective would it be. They would become much larger consumers as well as producers and thus the civilized world would be vastly benefited by the change, but none so much as China and Japan.

He also warned of the threat posed for the two countries by the Western powers:

U.S. Grant and China's Governor-General Li Hongzhang, 1879.

I can readily conceive that there are many foreigners, particularly among those interested in trade, who do not look beyond the present and who would like to have the present condition remain only grasping more from the east and leaving the natives of the soil merely "hewers of wood and drawers of water" for their benefit.

And this concern continued when Grant returned to the United States. Li Hongzhang maintained continual contact with Grant until his death. When the Qing government, worried about too much Western influence, was considering closing the Chinese Educational Mission, Grant, at the behest of Mark Twain, wrote a letter asking them to not do so. Li wrote Grant requesting that he tell the State Department to keep Charles Denby as U.S. legate in China. Grant also recommended to President Garfield in 1881 that he appoint Grant's friend, John Russell Young, who had accompanied him on his trip to the East and had documented it for the world, as U.S. Minister to Japan.

But it was President Chester Arthur—coming to the presidency after Garfield's agonizing death from an assassin's bullet—who in 1882 would appoint Young Minister to China, where he would help mediate the China-Japan relationship. Young played a major role in mediating the crisis between Japan and China over Korea. He remained until 1888, all the while doing his best to improve the relationship between the two countries.

Rediscovering America's Roots in the 20th Century

America's traditional and historic friendship with China would re-emerge in the course of the 20th century. The election of Franklin Roosevelt in 1932 empowered the spirit imbued with the American historical tradition of Lincoln and Grant. Franklin was a keen student of history; his great-great grandfather, Isaac Roosevelt, had been a collaborator of Alexander Hamilton.

Roosevelt's first two terms were almost fully occupied with pulling the country out of the Great Depression. Yet, it was also during those eight years that he initiated his Good Neighbor Policy with the nations of Latin America. The principle of this policy was non-interference and non-intervention in the domestic affairs of the Latin American countries. FDR reversed the previous "dollar diplomacy" programs, which had been

Hon. John Russell Young

brought in by his uncle Teddy Roosevelt, who became President following the 1901 assassination of President William McKinley. Franklin Roosevelt's policy was one of sovereignty, peace, and economic development, and later, during World War II, Roosevelt directed that the Good Neighbor Policy be used as the model for the post-war Bretton Woods monetary and economic agreements.

Looking forward to the post-war period, in which he felt he would play a crucial role in rebuilding a war-torn world, Roosevelt was intent on eliminating every vestige of underdevelopment and colonialism. On this he was in direct conflict with the British Prime Minister, Winston Churchill.

Roosevelt's son and aide, Elliott, gives the clearest picture of FDR's vision in his book, *As He Saw It*, based largely on the conversations he had with his father during the war. Elliott Roosevelt published this book in 1946, full of bitterness that FDR's successor, Harry

President Franklin Roosevelt and Prime Minister Winston Churchill, Yalta, February 4, 1945.

Truman, and his colleagues, had betrayed FDR's vision. Roosevelt had made clear to Churchill in Casablanca in 1944, that the British Empire would be dismantled, along with the French, the Dutch, and the Japanese empires. He was also insistent that the developing countries become independent, including British India, something Churchill would fight tooth and nail—unsuccessfully. Elliott Roosevelt noted that FDR was very clear to Churchill that the post-war world would not be ruled by Britain's colonial "18th-century methods" but by twentieth-century methods.

"Twentieth-century methods," Roosevelt told the Prime Minister, "involve bringing industry to these colonies. Twentieth-century methods include increasing the wealth of a people by increasing their standard of living, by educating them, by bringing them sanitation—by making sure they get a return for the raw wealth of their community."

In Roosevelt's plan, China would become one of the four major nations—with the United States, the Soviet Union, and Great Britain—to help keep the peace through their security cooperation. But after Roosevelt's death, even while the war in the Pacific was still underway, Churchill was in a position to gain control over the lightweight Harry Truman and launch the Cold War—and return most of the colonial overlords to power in their former colonies, on the pretext of "stopping communism."

Yet a similar Rooseveltian thrust would emerge fifteen years later with the election of President John F.

Kennedy. Chastened by the dangerous brinkmanship of the Cuban Missile Crisis, President Kennedy began to define a peace policy toward the Soviet Union, which he would elaborate most clearly in his famous speech at American University a few months before his death.

According to his friend and appointee, U.S. Ambassador to India John Kenneth Galbraith, once Kennedy had secured his second term, he intended to establish diplomatic relations with the People's Republic of China—a full seven years prior to Nixon's trip to China. During his last press conference on November 14, 1963, a week before he was murdered, Kennedy gave a hint of this when he was asked what his policy would be toward "Red China." Kennedy replied, "We are not wedded to a policy of hostility toward Red China," and added that to the extent that it normalized its relations with its neighbors, including India, the U.S. would be prepared to work with the People's Republic of China as well.

The Opportunity Today

China has now become the second most important economy in the world. With the background of its development from an impoverished nation to a relatively prosperous one, it is now working to help other countries to develop with its ambitious Belt and Road Initiative, and the United States has been invited to become a part of it. But this will only be possible if we can again revive the spirit of cooperation that so characterized our two nations' histories up until this point.

As economist and statesman Lyndon LaRouche has long underlined, the only "special relationship" that the United States should be part of is a four-power relationship among the United States, Russia, China and India, acting as partners, around which the rest of the world can orient in order to change the direction of economic development toward the type of infrastructural investment and win-win cooperation that has been so successfully laid out by China in its Belt and Road Initiative.

AUGUST 20, 2008

New Bretton Woods: Russia's Role in a Recovery[1]

by Lyndon H. LaRouche, Jr.

A fraudulent representation of the Franklin Roosevelt Bretton Woods system was recently launched at Modena, Italy, by a pair of seasoned turncoats, Jonathan Tennenbaum and Paolo Raimondi. The targets of their fully intended fraud included both important Russian scientists and notable Italian political figures. That pair of hoaxsters, who had gone over to the proverbial "other side" during recent years, represented a small, London-oriented circle of hoaxsters which have put themselves out for sale in search of hire and fame to be supplied by British Euro-oligarchical intelligence circles. The method by which that pair of hoaxsters perpetrated their fraud on the Russian and other guests, was passing themselves off, flagrantly, by representing themselves as being currently associated with me.

A significant number of participants in that Modena event have since expressed shock at discovering that fraud perpetrated upon them by the particular rascals Tennenbaum and Raimondi. The following report will serve, hopefully, as some compensation to them for the embarrassment which they suffered at the hands of that pair of hoaxsters.

Otherwise, the subject of the following pages of this report, has been posed to me by the way in which the relevant Russian participants, even including some prominent ones, were targeted for disinformation. The remedy for that abuse which they suffered on that account, is provided in the following pages, as a correction for the lack of understanding of Roosevelt's actual

Bretton Woods reform shown by the event's organizers. This correction by me will fill a gap in the knowledge of this matter among those present-day European policy shapers who were born after the close of the 1939-1945 general war. The object here is to make known the actual requirements for a present-day equivalent of the proposal which President Franklin D. Roosevelt initiated at the 1944 Bretton Woods conference.

The particular source of difficulty for some relevant Russian specialists, in particular, has been that they have often been victims of the errors of assumption of the type which might be expected as the net effect of an earlier, pro-Marxist indoctrination in the British imperialist monetary dogma of Adam Smith. Similarly, most Europeans of today, therefore tend to resist a competent understanding of the actual intention of President Franklin Roosevelt, and are not informed of the relevance of that Leibnizian science of physical economy which underlies the design of the Hamiltonian credit-system on which President Roosevelt's intentions had depended.

It is therefore important that these matters be clarified by me, not only for the benefit of Russians, but also most other patriotic Europeans, and also prominent North and South Americans of today. Economics is the one subject which is outstanding in the respect that everyone practices it, but almost no one in government around the world today has an actual understanding of what it is, in its effect, that they are actually practicing.

Foreword: The Dollar Is Still Mighty

But, not almighty.

The clearest example of the need for the kind of reform of the presently, hopelessly bankrupt world monetary-financial system which the world needs today, is to be recognized in the immediate problems

---

1. In part, the content of this publication overlaps the discussion in my recent June 12, 2008 "The Economic Debate About Russia" *EIR*, July 4, 2008. That earlier report should be referenced for its treatment of the historical background for the same economic issues during the 18th and 19th Centuries.

President Franklin Roosevelt intended to establish a new world order, at the end of World War II, based on the principle of Westphalia. His intention to eliminate all forms of imperialism, and to bring Russia into the community of nations, made Churchill apoplectic; FDR's plans were scrapped by his successor, Anglophile President Harry Truman. Stalin, Roosevelt, and Churchill are shown here at the wartime Tehran Conference, November 1943.

Furthermore, while it were desirable that any among Russia, China, India, and other nations would press the United States to initiate the New Bretton Woods reform which I have proposed, it is absolutely indispensable that that reform in international institutions actually be initiated as a proffer from the U.S.A. The reasons for that indispensable role of the U.S.A. lie, not only in the fact that "dollar" means "the big debt of the world system;" it also means, that only the U.S.A. Constitution provides the mechanism readily at hand by which a needed quality of New Bretton Woods system could be actually launched as an international treaty organization.

The obvious sort of likely objection to what I have just said, would be expressed by the question: "What if the U.S.A. were not to utter such an offer?"

Even if proposals for a "New Bretton Woods" from Russia, China, and India, could not be successful without U.S. concurrence, the making of those proposals *in the spirit of the Westphalian principle*, by those and other nations, will have a powerful, perhaps indispensable effect in pushing the U.S.A. toward launching the required initiative for joint action.

The only competent reply to that question which many might pose, would be, that the failure to push through this reform now, would mean that we shall all either actually go to the Hell which we will have brought upon ourselves, or, will be subjecting several coming generations of this planet as a whole to a roughly comparable effect. Thus, the campaign for a "new Bretton Woods," is one of those battles, like that of a great war already in progress, in which no acceptable choice but that either a Westphalian victory in policy is adopted, or the planet has already entered a new dark age.

Sometimes, as in physical-scientific practice, nature itself confronts us with choices like that: For this occasion, governments better decide to do it in a timely fashion, or those nation-states themselves may not be around long enough to be free to search for alternatives. Liberals of that general type which the excellent Eng-

which the recent collapse of the U.S. dollar represents for China. It is a China without whose participation no successful reform of what is the already bankrupt world system, could be managed by any part of the world at this time.

Simply restated, that challenge to be faced in capitals around the world today, is: "What about the U.S. dollar-denominated debts to China?" Without a system of parity based on approximately current physical content of U.S. dollars held as claims by China, no successful recovery from the present world economic breakdown-crisis would be possible. Without a reform of the type which requires the kind of cooperation I have specified for the initiation by the U.S.A., Russia, India, and China, there is no possibility of avoiding an already onrushing plunge of the planet as a whole, into a prolonged new dark age of all humanity.

lish patriot Jonathan Swift ridiculed, do not, admittedly, accept such notions of scientific imperatives with the good grace shown by such predecessors and patrons of Benjamin Franklin as Massachusetts' Increase and Cotton Mather. So, in the case that the Anglo-Dutch Liberal legacy of Paolo Sarpi were to prevail again today, mankind might be left with no hopeful option but to look for some future, perhaps distant time, when the self-elimination of the modern Sophistry of Liberalism from the human equation, provides mankind a poor and painful, but necessary relief from what has become the infinitely tiresome, continued existence of the moral depravity known as the Sarpian mode of Anglo-Dutch Liberalism.

The particular problem in today's world, is that the Trans-Atlantic world, especially in the northern hemisphere, has undergone a form and degree of moral and scientific degeneration since about 1968, in which competent knowledge of the physical and related requirements of a successful form of economy is, presently, rarely possessed or desired among that specifically white-collar, philosophically Liberal generation of the so-called "Baby Boomers," which was born between the 1945 close of the most recent world war, and the 1958 approach toward the so-called 1962 "missiles crisis."

In short, it is time for many nations to actually grow up, suddenly, to true adulthood. Admittedly, the dollar has been greatly depreciated since July 31, 1971; but, the potential of that dollar as a reserve currency remains unique, even if—for the present moment—the U.S.A. no longer actually owns it.

1. Ask China!

An increasing number of relevant officials, inside and outside China, recognize the global situation to which I have just referred; however, no governmental source on record known to me has shown, so far, a true comprehension of both the urgently needed warnings, and proposed remedies which I have uttered on this account. The problem is not that I have not been accurate, nor that I have lacked necessary precision on this subject-matter; *the problem is a familiar type of problem in present and past history alike. Many simply did not wish to hear of any rational change contrary to their own, passionately held, present prejudices.* This reality

can be studied as a composite of several historically defined issues of policy-making and, in general, the true history of tragedy in the planet's great affairs of today.

1. First of all, there is the matter of widespread ignorance, even among putative experts, of the fundamental difference in scientific principle, between the U.S. Constitution's specification of a credit-system, and a typical, usury-based, European monetary system.

2. Second, the vicious, cardinal error of substituting a monetarist standard for physical values.

3. The absence of a scientifically competent standard for defining "earned" profit margins, a standard needed to rid the current practice of financial accounting of its corrupting traditions of usury.

4. The failure to bring the notion of economy up to date, scientifically, in terms of the notions of Biosphere and Noösphere.

So, therefore, in this present report, we must, first, dispose of a widespread ignorance of the implications of the strategic conflict between the Bretton Woods System as it had been intended by President Franklin Roosevelt during the 1944 Bretton Woods conference, the conflict between Roosevelt's *anti-imperialist credit-system*, and the opposite, pro-imperialist intention expressed under that scoundrel President Harry S Truman, during the years which followed. Most of the present discussion to date, under the rubric of "New Bretton Woods System," implicitly accepts the axiomatic assumptions of the British opposition to President Roosevelt's actual intention, the opposition represented by the pro-imperialist, Keynesian, monetarist model. That was the mistaken model supported by both President Harry Truman and his British accomplices, in specific, systemic opposition to President Roosevelt's 1944 intention, during the years immediately following Roosevelt's death.

Some History To Be Considered

The new system, required to rescue the real economies from what are in fact the presently hopelessly bankrupt present systems, must earmark the elements which are to be saved, out of nominal values from the present, bankrupt systems, while discarding the remainder. The earmarked elements from *the discarded monetary systems*, must then be assimilated into *the new credit systems*.

As President Roosevelt stated clearly to Winston Churchill and others, during the course of the 1939-1945 world war, not only had the U.S. economic recovery under Roosevelt produced the most powerful economic war-machine the world had ever known. Roosevelt intended to use that available economic power to eliminate imperialism from the planet's forthcoming, post-war history.

Roosevelt's intention, including that expressed by his role in Bretton Woods, was that each nation must have true sovereignty under the needed new reforms, and, at the same time, that all forms of colonialism and its like must be uprooted from the planet. To that end, Roosevelt intended that the colonies should be freed to become truly sovereign nations. To accomplish this, he intended, that the physical-economic power of the U.S. war-machine would be converted into an instrument of a post-war order, an order in which all people would gain both political freedom from actual or virtual colonial status, and each nation would be assisted in the economic development needed to sustain that sovereignty.

These had been the anti-imperialist intentions which Roosevelt had stated clearly, and repeatedly, to Winston Churchill and other relevant figures during the interval of the 1939-1945 war. Had President Roosevelt lived through the end of that war, those intentions were about to be fulfilled, but only if Roosevelt's 1944 design for Bretton Woods were carried forward at the point of the coming close of the war. This intention by him has been supported, continually, by me, as my expressed intention in all the recent forty years of my life as a public political figure, and in all my designs for public policy, over all of the past four decades, to present date.

For example: the actual source of all of the actually important opposition to the role which I have played in public affairs during these decades, has been an echo of the leading opponents of that Franklin Roosevelt legacy, opponents who represented the same political species of powerful trans-Atlantic financier interests against which President Franklin Roosevelt had fought up to the moment of his death, an intention, by him, which I have been proud to serve.

What I affirm for today as this continuing intention for the post-war world, had been the foundation for President Roosevelt's launching of a fixed-exchange-rate *credit-system* at the 1944 Bretton Woods conference.

FDR's Intended Principle

What President Roosevelt had intended, as I do today, is not some new, vulgar mercantilist contract among competing separate powers, but a reform of the world's economic and related affairs according to a single, commonly adopted great principle, one conceived in the same spirit as the 1648 Peace of Westphalia. What is required, if civilization today is to be rescued from its own pervasive folly, is a submission to a common universal principle, as it were to be conceived as an adopted principle of nature, as was that Peace of Westphalia. It must become a new, refreshed body of *anti-monetarist,*[2] *natural, international law of economy, binding together a system of respectively perfectly sovereign nation-states by a common, universal principle adopted in the likeness of a universal physical principle.* Either those nations will bind themselves together according to that principle, or the case for each and all among them would be a hopeless cause.[3]

Thus, although the U.S.A.'s alliance with Britain was necessary for the defeat of Hitler's power at that time, it was a very difficult alliance between a sovereign nation-state and an empire, as President Roosevelt, General Douglas MacArthur, General Dwight Eisenhower, and others saw clearly during that time of war. For just that reason, the continued existence of President Franklin Roosevelt was, therefore, seen by London as a grave strategic threat to the continued, post-war existence of the British Empire. For that reason, the death of President Roosevelt was seized as the strategic opportunity which Britain desperately desired, the opportunity to corrupt and ruin the post-Franklin Roosevelt U.S.A., as we should be able to see this clearly in retrospect today.

For reason of those war-time circumstances, President Roosevelt made difficult alliances with such circles from among both his domestic and foreign opposition during the war-time; this was done in order to secure the launching and needed continuing support for

2. I.e., anti-monetarist, anti-Keynes.
3. The lack of this specific type of binding common principle, was the specific, potentially fatal error pervading the agreements made among the participants lured into the trap at Modena.

Gen. Dwight Eisenhower, Supreme Commander of the Allied Forces in Europe during the Second World War, shared FDR's view that an alliance with Britain was necessary for the defeat of Hitler, but understood the difference between the American and British systems. Truman, on the other hand, acted as a British tool, following FDR's death. Eisenhower and Truman are shown here at an airfield in Brussels, July 1945.

the war from among the Wall Street and like-minded factions within the U.S.A. So, already, as soon as the U.S.-led forces had succeeded in breaking through the Normandy beachhead, the right-wing supporters of the war in the U.S., unleashed a campaign against Roosevelt in concert with the relevant circles in the British establishment. Among President Roosevelt's most difficult concessions to his political adversaries within the Anglo-American camp, had been the replacement of Vice-President Wallace by his right-wing Democratic Party adversary Senator Harry Truman for the 1944 nomination of a U.S. Vice-President.

For example:

As soon as the Allied breakthrough at Normandy had been completed, the British imperialists, and their sympathizers in the U.S.A., took measures, such as the catastrophic "Market Garden" swindle led by British Field Marshal Montgomery, to prolong the warfare unnecessarily, by operations which would prevent an otherwise available completion of the mission of that war by the close of 1944.[4] Similarly, the British betrayal of

the German Generals' Plot against the Nazi regime was a betrayal made to prevent such a relatively immediate cessation of warfare. The militarily absurd and immoral, British-led terror-bombings of non-military civilian targets, such as Dresden and Magdeburg, were also typical of post-Normandy British objectives of this same Churchillian character.

We have seen the same British imperial policy of late 1944 and early 1945 in the post-1989 actions by Britain's Prime Minister Margaret Thatcher and her asset François Mitterrand, to dismember and loot a reunited Germany and also ruin the nations of the eastern European Comecon and the former Soviet Union itself, a looting continued up to the first inauguration of Vladimir Putin as the new President of Russia.

The foolish acquiescence of most Presidents, and most Congresses of the U.S.A.,[5] like some other nations, to these recurring British imperial policies of practice, has transformed the two decades since the beginning of 1989, into one of the most monstrous destructions of physical productive potential, and essential basic economic infrastructure, in places such as Europe and North America, in modern history.

This deliberate ruin of the U.S. economy had begun

---

4. Back during the late 1980s, when I asked a leading international law specialist who conducted the rear-guard retreat of Field Marshal Rommel from El-Alamein, if he agreed with my estimate that Montgomery was the worst commander of an army in World War II, he laughed, and replied: "I was leading the rear guard for Rommel all the way to Tunis; if Montgomery ever flanked me, I would be dead today. I am very grateful to Montgomery; he saved my life." Montgomery, among his other strategic incompetencies, was a raving anti-African racist. However, there is no doubt that the replacement, in Egypt, of competent British commanders by Montgomery fulfilled the intention of Prime Minister Churchill, that the war in Europe not be won "too soon."

5. The most disgusting case of the ruinous capitulation of the Congress and the political parties occurred from January 2006, onward, through British pressures on party leaderships exerted through the pro-fascist Felix Rohatyn of Lazard Frères pedigree, and the British Foreign Office's predator George Soros. This actually began during the Spring of 2005, at a time when the Congress had responded positively to my pushing for defense of the Social Security system, but when the Congress had already capitulated, under Rohatyn's pressure, from Springtime on, not to prevent the liquidation of the last bastion of U.S. agro-industrial might, the auto industry. Hardly a patriotic sort of behavior by the leaders of the Congress.

with President Truman. The death of President Roosevelt, had already cleared the way for a fundamental change, carried out by President Truman, in full witting service of the British (e.g., "Anglo-American") imperial interest, in the mission-orientation assigned to what emerged as the International Monetary Fund (IMF). The evidence of the intention of that change was immediate. The former colonies which had been marked for independence, during President Roosevelt's term, were now doomed to various forms of either their former, colonial status (such as Indo-China and Indonesia), or some thinly disguised form of pseudo-independence under Anglo-Dutch Liberal financier control of all important moveable assets of those newly "freed" nations.

Thus, instead of a global political and economic reconstruction of the post-war world, the mass of U.S. agro-industrial potential available through conversion of military-industrial-agricultural capabilities to civilian development of the economies of the world, was either largely wasted, or, otherwise, was reoriented from the intention under Franklin Roosevelt, to establishing what is sometimes identified as a neo-colonialist system, under which what should be the emerging, economically developing nations, were prevented from enjoying "too much liberty" in developing their national resources and productivity per capita and per square kilometer. The presently continuing, pro-genocidal victimization of Africa under British imperial overlordship, has been, to the present moment in world history, among the most shameful expressions of this brutishness under the Keynesian alternative to Roosevelt's intended credit-system policies.

London's Treasonous U.S. Assets

We must never forget such examples from the rise of Anglo-Dutch imperialism, as the British use of its puppets of the Nineteenth-Century Spanish monarchy to build up African slavery in the post-1815-war United States, and also that monarchy's assistance to the British in corrupting and wrecking the Ibero-American states of South and Central America. These things were done as a conscious form of warfare, directed under the British Foreign Office's Jeremy Bentham and his protege Lord Palmerston.

Nor must we forget the Anglo-Dutch Liberal interest's earlier creation of the Seven Years War as the means by which British imperialism ruined continental Europe to London's strategic advantage. Nor must we forget the warning stated by Germany's Chancellor Bismarck, that the general war on the continent of Europe being prepared by Britain's Prince Edward Albert, already during the 1890s, was intended to be the "geo-political" intention of Britain's second, imperial "Seven Years War."

All of the major warfare on this planet since the 1890 ouster of impediment Bismarck from the Chancellory, as in Edward Albert's launching Japan into its 1895-1945 warfare against China, and as every major war on this planet since 1895, has been a continuation of the same strategic principle expressed by Edward Albert's use of the model of the Anglo-Dutch Liberal conduct of the Seven Years War, a principle continued in such forms as the crucial role of Britain's Prime Minister Tony Blair in plunging the U.S.A. into U.S. President George W. Bush, Jr.'s foolish, fraudulently conceived, wasting warfare in Southwest Asia , a terrible chaos not only continuing, but spreading, now, with the complicity of President George W. Bush, Jr.'s administration, into Pakistan, up to the present moment this present report of mine is written.

Thus, we see in these examples from modern British history since the 1763 Peace of Paris, that men and women rarely live to 100 years, but that nations' and empires' cultures and habits often span centuries.

Was Truman a Traitor?

From the very day after President Roosevelt's most untimely death, London's asset Truman was already serving as the British Empire's ally against the intended policies of the Bretton Woods system.

This presents thoughtful historians with a certain question: *Was President Truman therefore a traitor?* In U.S. tradition, excepting extreme cases such as one-time U.S. Vice-President Aaron Burr, such tainted political figures are not formally considered to be traitors, but rather as political skunks or, worse, like creatures such as former U.S. Vice-President Al Gore from "Possum Hollow," Gore, for example. Gore today typifies a certain kind of ambiguous, in-between place, which Gore shares with British assets such as U.S. Presidents Andrew "Slippery" Jackson and with Jackson's controller, and traitor Aaron Burr's successor on Wall Street, Martin van Buren, and John Quincy Adams' and Abraham Lincoln's adversary, Polk, later. Van Buren was the author of the scheme, installed by his puppet and "Trail of Tears" veteran Jackson, which exploded as the financial Panic (banking) of 1837.[6] Theodore Roosevelt and Ku Klux Klan backer Woodrow Wilson, or Coolidge, Richard Nixon, and other Presidents of a kindred stripe, later, were similar cases of corruption.

So, where President Roosevelt's administration had marked former colonies for liberation, the British Empire, working hand-in-glove with Truman, had restored either old colonial rule in other places, or imposed new guises for the same thing, in effect, as in the presently continuing British population-control policy for the looting of the African continent, which was also adopted by the U.S.A. under Ford and Carter during the middle through late 1970s.

The Spring 1945 change in U.S. policy, from Roosevelt to Truman, had thus produced a corresponding trend of change in the content and meaning of the name "Bretton Woods system." That change in meaning of the term, under Truman, has been a principal source of the present general confusion among the misinformed (and those who wish to appear to be misinformed), world wide, respecting both the Franklin Roosevelt legacy in particular, and the American System of political-economy in general.

Therefore, it is essential to focus here on *the specific difference in principle* between President Franklin Roosevelt's Bretton Woods intention of 1944, the establishment of an international Bretton Woods credit-system, and Truman's perversion of Roosevelt's policy, to use the name of the 1944 Bretton Woods draft as a cover for a fixed-exchange-rate monetarist system premised on the imperialist monetarist dogma of John Maynard Keynes.

Roosevelt Versus Keynes

To understand today's global economic crisis, we must see the stark contrast of the system of uttering of money defined by the U.S. Federal Constitution, to the usual European monetary systems, the British system. We must trace the underlying consistency of trends of change, away from President Franklin Roosevelt's intention, a change which has not only ruined what had

Orange County, Calif. Fire Ant Authority

The monarchy of the British, or Anglo-Dutch Liberal system of international usury, and its swarm of private financiers, can best be compared to a swarm of ants, in which a reigning queen can be replaced, but the character of the swarm as an institution persists. Shown, a queen ant surrounded by workers and brood.

been the most powerful and productive economy the world had ever known, to the state of wreckage to which it has been degraded today. It has been a wrecking-process which began with the inauguration of President Harry Truman and his Anglo-American policy of imperialist re-colonization of many among the nations of the poorer peoples of the world, as that same ugly policy of the British empire is deployed against Sudan, Zimbabwe, and other nations of Africa today.

To begin the needed exploration of this relevant matter of recent history, consider, briefly, the essential, principled difference between the British system and that of the United States Constitution, a difference which is of crucial significance for anyone who seeks to benefit from the legacy of the Bretton Woods system.

Under the U.S. Federal Constitution, the creation of money is a monopoly of the elected Federal Executive, but this is permitted only under the condition of the consent of the lower house of the U.S. Congress. This consent is the authorization to create a specific debt of the Federal Government, which is put into circulation as an increase of money authorized to be put into circulation through the U.S. Treasury directly, or through credit extended for authorized loans through such institutions as U.S. Federal and state chartered banks, or through treaty-agreements with foreign nations to which the U.S. Congress has consented.

What I have proposed as the treaty-organization to be launched through the joint initiative of the U.S.A.,

---

6. Burr was an asset of Lord Shelburne's lackey Jeremy Bentham, who headed the British Foreign Office's Secret Committee. Bentham ran the Foreign Office's operations in France from 1782-83 on, and produced his principal successor Lord Palmerston. He controlled Burr totally.

Russia, China, and India, is an outstanding example of the advantages available for the use of a credit system, rather than a monetary system of the Keynesian type.

The British monetarist system, is derived from the tradition of an ancient system of usury, as practiced in the Mediterranean and adjoining regions over the course of ancient, medieval, and modern times. The prevalent modern European parliamentary systems were derived from the practice of concessions to the medieval and modern Venetian systems of tyranny through usury. The medieval Crusades have been the model used for such operations as the presently, London-steered, ongoing wasting wars and related terrorist operations in Southwest Asia. The contemporary Anglo-Dutch Liberal system, for example, was an outgrowth of the reforms by that New Venetian Party of Paolo Sarpi, which moved the bulk of intrinsically usurious, Venetian financier operations from the Mediterranean littoral, to the maritime regions of the northern coastal regions of Europe, that with increasing emphasis on maritime usury (e.g., Adam Smith, "buy cheap and sell dear") practiced in the realm of transoceanic traffic.

The essential difference between the two systems, American versus British, American System versus John Maynard Keynes, et al., is that *the American System is based on a constitutional principle of public credit*, where the Anglo-Dutch Liberal system, including its Keynesian variant, is based on an implicitly imperialist, reigning law of usury, a reign of private money established as the hereditary benefit delivered to a predatory, financier class. The latter is a system under which citizens and their governments pay tribute to the power of privately held hoards of financial assets, an intrinsically predatory Adam Smith system, under which people are cheap, and under which usurious profit-taking, by means of the swindles concocted by the private money-interest, is dear.

Under the American System, the constitutional system supported by President Franklin Roosevelt, *Federal public credit*, as defined by our Constitution, is supreme, and the Federal government exerts the power of regulation, through the instrument of public credit, as also coinage, throughout the land.

The British system, of which the Keynesian system is a subsumed variant, is more accurately labeled "the Anglo-Dutch Liberal system of international usury." Under that monetarist system, the private financier-oligarchical interest loots the public credit, supremely. The modern monarchies themselves are predominantly Liberal Venetians of the Sarpi pedigree, sometimes dressed up with feudal trappings, but despite such costumed buffoonery, are actually very, very "bourgeois" monarchies, and are representatives of the collective interest embodied in the swarm of private financiers, as it were the "Queen" of the hornets' nest. Sometimes, the swarm of hornets, or of ants, may dump a reigning queen, and replace her with another government, but the character of the swarm as an institution persists. The essence of the business lies in the relationship of the hive to what it deems its lawful prey, the ordinary citizen or the like.

The actual British Empire of today, for example, is, in every systemic cultural and other leading feature, an outgrowth of the influence of both Sarpi's reforms, and the earlier Venetian slaughter of statesmen and royal wives under the reign of mad Henry VIII. The empire itself is essentially a financial empire based on usury, rather than being a secretion of the will of the population of the British Isles; that is the essential meaning of "free trade" (free of government interference with usury and kindred swindles). With the combination of the shutting down of the U.S.-based Bretton Woods system, under U.S. President Nixon, in 1971-72, with the great Anglo-Dutch-Saudi petroleum-hoax swindle of 1973, and with the breakdown of the U.S. economic system carried out by David Rockefeller and his cronies under the rubric of the Trilateral Commission, the U.S. economy has been systematically looted and wrecked.

This wrecking has been done almost as much from the inside as from the the actions of the Anglo-Dutch-Saudi operations centered in the petroleum spot-market operations and the BAE (e.g., El Yamamah). This vast petroleum swindle, combined with London-centered "protection" of a vast international narcotics trafficking, has taken over control of the U.S. and the U.S. dollar system, beginning with those radical measures of destruction of the U.S. economic system during the implicitly treasonous interval between pressure on President Johnson to capitulate to the British on the U.S. dollar, on March 1, 1968, and the subsequent, 1981 inauguration of President Ronald Reagan.[7]

---

7. Some have argued, in the past, and would probably still insist today, that the January-February 1968 crisis of the dollar was a product of the U.S. expenditures for Indo-China warfare, up to that point. That crisis was actually, predominantly, a side-effect of a fraudulently crafted (i.e., the Gulf of Tonkin resolution) launching of war in Indo-China. That popular view of the February 1968 dollar-crisis overlooks two most crucial sets of facts. First, that the 1968 dollar-crisis was an echo of British

Library of Congress

EIRNS/Stuart Lewis

The intention of the U.S. Constitution was identified by the first Secretary of the Treasury Alexander Hamilton, in his three reports to the U.S. Congress during 1790-1791: The efficacy of Hamilton's policies was "borne out beyond reasonable doubt" over the course of the history of the U.S. economy since that time to the present date. Shown: the First Bank of the U.S., Philadelphia; statue of Hamilton at the U.S. Treasury Building in Washington.

If we select attention to these, subsequent 1968-1981 developments, and their 1981-2008 sequel of today, what has happened to the post-Franklin Roosevelt U.S.A. has been a relatively successful period of continued net physical growth of the U.S. economy over the interval 1945-1967. We see a significant slowing of that progress during the 1964-1967 years. This was followed by an uninterrupted period of increasing rate of net collapse of the *physical economy*, per capita and per square kilometer, during the course of the forty-

year net physical collapse, 1968-2008. Statistics which have been forged to suggest a contrary, post-1968 effect, have been clearly fraudulent concealment of the visible physical reality of the increasing ruin of the general population and territory of the U.S.A. under the cover of financial jiggery-pokery crafted for the intellectual consumption of the credulous.

The three factors which have had the greatest impact in forcing the long wave of collapse of the physical output of the U.S. economy, per capita and per square kilometer, over the 1968-2008 interval, have been the net collapse of production and maintenance of basic economic infrastructure which began in fiscal year 1967-1968, the establishment of the combination of President Nixon's wrecking the last remnant of the Bretton Woods system in August 1971, and systemic wrecking of every pillar of progress in our system through the injection of the policies of the David Rockefeller-Brzezinski Trilateral Commission, beginning the U.S. Carter Administration.

In the following five chapters of this report, I trace more of the implications of the four subject-matters listed in the opening of this present chapter.

Prime Minister Harold Wilson's collapse of the British Pound. That collapse of the Pound, itself, had been the fruit of a Wilson Labour Government policy of wrecking the industrial economy of the United Kingdom from the beginning of that Wilson government's takeover of power through an orchestrated Profumo scandal against the Macmillan government. Wilson's economic-wrecking policies were the forerunner of the economic-wrecking policies of the Nixon, Ford, and Carter administrations, especially by the Carter Administration's implementation of the Trilateral Commission lunacy. The policy of the British establishment since the death of Franklin Roosevelt, had been to wreck the U.S.A.'s role as a leading power through a policy of what is called the Malthusian "environmentalism" of Britain's Prince Philip and ex-Waffen-SS official Prince Bernhard of the Netherlands, and Bertrand Russell's Wellsian program for World Government.

2. Why a Credit-System?

1. First of all, there is the matter of widespread ignorance, even among putative experts, of the fundamental difference in scientific principle, between the U.S. Constitution's specification of a credit-system, and a typical, usury-based, European monetary system.

The intention of the Constitution of the United States was identified by the original U.S. Secretary of the Treasury, Alexander Hamilton, under three reports to the U.S. Congress during 1790-1791: ***Report on Public Credit*** (1790), ***Report on a National Bank*** (1790), and ***Report on the Subject of Manufactures*** (1791).

These policies respecting currency and related matters, were, in principle, enacted into U.S. Constitutional law under, principally, *Sections §7* and *§8* of *Article I* of the original ***U.S. Federal Constitution.*** Although some founders, such as Jefferson, were opposed to the ***National Bank*** and to some among the implications of Hamilton's ***Report on the Subject of Manufactures,*** both of these policies emphasized by Hamilton were borne out beyond reasonable doubt by the comparative evidence of the contending impulses for enforcement of, and failure to implement those principles, over the course of the total history of the U.S. economy since that time to the present date.

The ideas on which these constitutional policies were premised then, and later, were drawn from the very roots of modern European history, as reflected in such publications,on the subject of the sovereign nation-state as Dante Alighieri's ***De Monarchia*** and Cardinal Nicholas of Cusa's ***Concordancia Catholica,*** and, on the principles of physical economy codified by Cusa, as in his founding of the principles of modern physical science in his ***De Docta Ignorantia.*** The first modern nation-state premised on Cusa's principles of statecraft and physical economy, was that of France's Louis XI. The imitation of Louis XI's successful example by England's Henry VII, established the precedent on which all successful modern European models of statecraft in general, and economy, are models of early success to the present day.

The effort, organized by the Venetian financier oligarchy, to attempt to crush the accomplishments of the great 1438-1439 ecumenical Council of Florence, beginning the Fall of Constantinople, was the precedent for what became the same Venetian party's direction of the religious warfare which dominated and wracked European civilization from the 1492 expulsion of the Jews from Spain until the adoption of the great 1648 Peace of Westphalia.

The 1492-1648 interval of a Europe dominated by religious warfare, was succeeded by a relatively brief interval of the crucial 1620-1688 colonization of a New England led by the Winthrops and Mathers. By 1689, the great rise of the Commonwealth of Massachusetts had been crushed, and many relevant New England families subjected to a long-ranging process of corruption. The party of the Winthrops and Mathers struggled on at their posts, but even they soon advised figures such as the later leading American scientist and statesman, Benjamin Franklin, to shift the base of their party's operations to the Pennsylvania of James Logan et al. For a great moment of history, during the first decade of the Eighteenth Century, the great universal intellect of Gottfried Leibniz challenged the enemies of a civilized form of society; but, then, the defeat of the English Tory faction of Leibniz, Jonathan Swift, et al., by the accession of England's Liberals' regime of King George I, shifted the best hopes of the Europeans to the emerging potential for a republic along the shores of North America.[8]

Out of the success of the great struggles, centered then in the France of Cardinal Mazarin and Jean-Baptiste Colbert, came a great flourishing of science in the tradition of Nicholas of Cusa's avowed followers Leonardo da Vinci, Johannes Kepler, and also such among their Seventeenth-Century followers as Fermat, Pascal, Christiaan Huyghens, and Gottfried Leibniz. Thus, the great tradition of the Sixteenth-Century followers of Cusa, such as Leonardo da Vinci and Niccolo Machiavelli, and Cusa's and Leonardo's follower Johannes Kepler, created the foundations of the political state-

---

8. This orientation of the leading freedom-seeking circles of Europe to hope from the progress in North America persisted under the aftermath of the combined French Revolution and 1812-1815 swindle by Metternich and Jeremy Bentham's Treaty of Vienna. The rise of the U.S.A. under President Abraham Lincoln over Bentham's and Palmerston's launching of the Nineteenth-Century use of Spanish slave-trade as a strategic operation into the U.S. territory, restored this orientation of European hopes from the rise of United States to a great power among nations. Otherwise, the ability of European oligarchical interests to prejudice European populations and others against the U.S.A. has been chiefly facilitated by the British role in backing the election and incumbencies of bad U.S. Presidents.

craft associated with the great ecumenical Council of Florence, embodied in those international circles centered in the figure and influence of the universal genius of Leibniz.

I emphasize here, again, that the special nature of the human individual, as distinct from all the beasts, and also, generally speaking, English-speaking Liberals, is that although man has the incarnate form of another beast, the creative potential lodged within the birth of the newborn human individual, expresses a potential immortality of the personal human identity of that individual who participates in the preservation of the uniquely human creative power of human individuals.[9] As I have emphasized, the human individual who lives up to that potential, does not lose his, or her viable identity with death of the mortal body. Rather, the good which the individual conveys is a power that has been proven by known history, and even earlier traces, to reach across many centuries, even millennia. It is the individual who accepts that noble destiny, who is among the true leaders from mankind's past, and in its future destiny.

Thus, the Preamble of the U.S. Federal Constitution states simply and nobly:

> We the people of the United States, in Order to form a more perfect Union, and to establish Justice, insure domestic Tranquility, provide for the common Defense, to promote the general Welfare, and secure the Blessings of Liberty to ourselves and our Posterity, do ordain and establish this Constitution for the United States of America.

This Constitution reflected the colonists' experience of the relevant great literature from ancient scientific and other sources which the Winthrops and the Mathers of the Seventeenth and Eighteenth centuries' colonization knew through their own education and that of their children and grandchildren. It embodied the great tradition of Cardinal Mazarin's leading role in organizing the great 1648 Peace of Westphalia, and the informed opinion which these North American colonists had formed through experience with the ever fresh eruptions of brutishness from the reigning powers of the continent, of Europe, especially the European aristocratic and financier oligarchies. During the course of the middle through late Eighteenth Century, Americans had come, partly through the radiated effect of the lead-

ing role of Benjamin Franklin as a publicist, to relatively up-to-date knowledge of important developments within Europe, and among the future states which were then the English colonies.

As the case of Leibniz himself attests to this, the most direct influence on the development of the culture of the North American colonies was that radiated, as by Gottfried Leibniz, from the France of Jean-Baptiste Colbert. It was the role and influence of Colbert in promoting the science-driven economic progress in the productive powers of labor in France, and the unprecedented degree of achievements accomplished in France under his personal influence, which informed the developing future states in North America. It was, for example, an example rooted in the precedents of Colbert's France, which prompted this North America to actually introduce the industrial revolution to mid-Eighteenth-Century England, not the reverse. The modernity of the Saugus Iron Works in Seventeenth-Century New England attests to the superiority of the progress of economy in New England relative to England under the Kings of that time.

It has been a popular, foolish belief among many poorly informed Europeans, and even some Americans, as shown in historical researches published by my associate Anton Chaitkin, that the initial advantages of the English-speaking colonies in North America came from looting of natural resources. Here, on this point, we encounter the roots, in day-to-day, and generation-to-generation experience, of the newly formed United States' keen appreciation of the advantages of its Constitutional credit-system over a monetary system, as opposed to an inherently usurious, neo-Venetian type of British or continental monetary system even today.

The impetus and character of development of the productive powers of labor in the English colonies of North America is well illustrated by the writing of my late associate, professional historian H. Graham Lowry's *How the Nation Was Won*.[10] The increase of the productive powers of labor is accomplished through credible promises of future physical basis for the generation of means of payment of that investment, that over not only years, but, often, successive generations.

This principle was understood very well by the

---

9. E.g., man's soul in the image of his Creator.

10. H. Graham Lowry, *How the Nation Was Won: America's Untold Story*, **pdf** https://store.larouchepub.com/product-p/eirbk-1988-1-0-0-pdf.htm **kindle** https://store.larouchepub.com/product-p/eirbk-1988-1-0-0-kindle.htm **epub** https://store.larouchepub.com/product-p/eirbk-1988-1-0-0-epub.htm (Washington, D.C.: Executive Intelligence Review, 1988).

EIRNS/Claudio Celani

Today's economic/financial meltdown can be fairly dated to Alan "Bubbles" Greenspan's chairmanship of the Federal Reserve Bank.

founder of the first modern European nation-state, France's Louis XI, who created a profit for France and its individuals of all classes through bribing English, Burgundian, and Spanish predators into peace, which allowed the productive powers of labor and means of production to be built up in France. The same wise practice of Louis XI was adopted by his admirer, England's Henry VII, thus creating both a France and an England which became the principal heralds of successive forms of modern nation-state economy and its marketing practices. This was the echo of a precious lesson from the development of large regions of future France and Germany under the leadership of Charlemagne, as the still living inland waterways of continental Europe attest to the present day.

A prudent economy is one which invests in the profit of its own people through the credit organized for that people by its own self-government. An excess of foreign loans, especially loans from predatory usurers in the Venetian tradition, is usually a sign, not of the lenders' hope of prompt repayment as scheduled, but their lust for the perpetually increasing indebtedness of the nation and its citizens to the alien predators such as those lenders themselves. Such are the predatory "Mr. Scratch" types of Felix Rohatyn and George Soros.[11]

---

11. "Mr. Scratch" was the name which author Stephen Vincent Benet assigned to the Satan of his famous, long short story, *The Devil and Daniel Webster*.

Decent foreign loans are those arranged among nations allied in common cause against predatory adversaries. As Popes of the past might have forewarned you: never trust a Venetian, especially when he is engaged in his customarily most evil role, pretending to be your friend and backer.

3. Why Physical Economy?

2. Second, the vicious, cardinal error of substituting a monetarist standard for physical values.

"When Adam delved and Eve span, who then was nobleman?"

For intelligent and sane economists, however rare they might be in this age of post-industrial decadence, the only competent policy for capital investment, is the reasonable presumption that the *physical* productive powers of labor of the national economy (and, implicitly, the world) will be increased as the fruit of that enterprise. It is not the ownership of property which defines this required accomplishment; it is the benefit expressed as the increase of the physical productive powers of labor, per capita and per square kilometer of national, and, implicitly, world territory.

This output of society is not to be counted as the summing-up of individual estimates of values, but as the effect of the whole process on the relative value of the process considered directly as an indivisible whole. *Is the potential relative population-density of the territory and population as a whole increased to a higher dynamic level (as a whole), or not?*

The notion of *physical* must, however, be congruent with certain implications of Academician V.I. Vernadsky's notions of the categorical (phase-spatial) distinctions of the abiotic, the Biosphere, and the Noösphere, as I shall identify those distinctions here.

The value of any particular part of that process is to be measured implicitly by the effect of the removal, or addition of the examined element from, or to the whole process as a process, not an aggregate of separate things.

Therefore, the object of pricing is to provide a reasonable estimate of the relative price, one which corresponds to the physical value of the particular as a functional part of the whole, as better defined in those terms.

As a matter of contrasts, the good workman, or the

The pro-Satanic dogma of the likes of Al Gore, and his British royal masters Princes Charles and Philip, is based on their worship of entropy. Their hatred of scientific progess, e.g., nuclear power, expresses their devotion to the image of Aeschylus' Olympian Zeus. Left to right: Gore, Charles, Philip.

honest entrepreneur, seeks to leave behind a condition of the world which is better, by these standards for physical investment, than it had been when he, or she had entered that world. *Without such a notion of progress, there is no truthful notion of economic value.* The sense of a practical quality of personal immortality expressed in this fashion, is typical of the human individual who thinks, with reference to such physical terms, about the kind of world which his, or her, life will leave behind him. Under the real conditions of today's onrushing, global breakdown-crisis, there is, morally, no allowable room for defining "investment" in the terms of the delusionary folly of "marginal utilities."

Those so summarized considerations, respecting the economic processes of entire nations as wholes, are the essence of the matter from the standpoint of a physical-scientific outlook.

The principles for adducing the relative prices which are approximately congruent, in effect, with those physical values, is a matter of the good approximations necessary for conducting local financial transactions within the economy considered as a whole process.

Any contrary definition of productive investment, is chiefly a matter of the folly popular among the monetarist entrepreneurs and their male or female mistresses. Lusty satisfaction, in one way or another, by the person, has become the often sado-masochistic motive of the typical actual, or would-be capitalist.

Consider some relatively commonplace, or false opinions on the subject of economic value. For example:

Why Both Al Gore & Satan Are Wrong

One among the present prototypes of the religious dogma of service to Satan and his followers, is that essentially pro-Satanic dogma of the likes of former Vice-President Al Gore: his worship of entropy. I mean their opposition to the conceptual outlook of a science-driven, physical-economic development of national physical economies, their opposition, such as that of Gore and his masters, England's Princes Philip and Charles, to the up-shifting of modes of productive existence to higher levels of effective energy-flux density, as by nuclear power, expresses their implicit devotion to the pro-Satanic image of Aeschylus' Olympian Zeus. That expresses, thus, notions comparable in effect of practice to those of Hitlerian depravity. This is as shown by their denial of the right to physical development of the continental nations of Africa by Africans, a denial which is among the frankest expression of that counter-productive trio's share of investment in moral depravity.

For example: the essential common character of Gore and Princes Philip and Charles, is their defiance of the scientific reality of what the late Academician V.I. Vernadsky defined as the Biosphere and Noösphere. We shall return to that matter later in this report, but, for the moment, the following clarification of the point is sufficient for the purposes of the discussion immediately at hand in this present chapter.

During the course of the preceding century, any competent approach to economic science recognizes that the mass of the planet Earth is composed of three distinct types of products.

First, is the portion of that physical mass whose adduced origin is pre-biotic (derived from non-living origins. Only life generates life.

Second, that the product of the mass of living processes and the products, as residues, is, thus, specific to living, or formerly living creatures.

Third, is the portion of the mass of the planet which is the increased product of nothing other than the activity of human beings, human beings who are set categorically apart from the beasts by their innate, creative-mental (noëtic) abilities to make, and to employ discoveries of physical principle willfully, discoveries through which the human species can increase its potential relative population-density, per capita and per square kilometer, as no other living species of marsupial or mammal could do this.

If there ever were an actual Mephistopheles of Marlowe's and Goethe's fancy, he were certainly a suitable model for Venice's Paolo Sarpi, whose dogma has been the unifying basis for Anglo-Dutch Liberalism, up through the present day. Here, Mephistopheles appears before Faust, in a lithograph by Eugène Delacroix, 1828.

The distinction of one among these categories from the others, is located in the existence of relevant, corresponding physical principles. Thus, as emphasized in the opening of this present chapter, the principle of life is a universal physical principle of a phase-space, whereas the principle of human creativity is a universal physical principle of another phase-space. The common product is therefore to be found in the dynamics of the interaction of the three phase-spaces: the "inorganic," the Biosphere, and the Noösphere.

These just-identified conclusions are evident in the comparison of the fossil masses of human beings, and non-human living processes, to the known abiotic mass of our planet and the Moon, and related evidence of the Solar System at large. Life, thus, is a principle of the universe which is not derived from non-life, while the mass of the planet specific to human life and its unique products, expresses a principle associated with the notion of human individual creativity, which does not exist among any other known form of existence. The order among these three categories, is that life increases its share of the mass of the planet at the expense of non-life, whereas the human species increases its share relative to all lower forms of living processes.

The idea of a reasonable estimate of physical-eco-nomic value, is to be crafted from the standpoint of the role of the Noösphere as the highest level of outcome of the dynamic interaction of the three phase-spaces.

Thus, since any fixed mode of social existence of mankind tends to outrun the depletable resources of non-human masses, only the quality of development of human *noëtic* powers, as expressed typically by the quality of scientific and related progress unique to the individual member of the human species, permits the indefinitely continued existence of mankind's national cultures, on this planet (or, beyond).

The living purpose of the form of existence to be chosen by mankind, is that typified as the scientific and related qualities of anti-entropic progress associated with the development of societies through increasingly capital-intensive, technologically revolutionary progress in what we call "labor by individual persons." Productive labor governed by a principle of anti-entropic, increasingly capital-intensive (physically) progress, is the inherent destiny which the Creator has assigned implicitly to mankind.

The effect of the act of individual human creativity is typified by the individual's discovery, or reenacting of the discovery of a relevant universal physical principle, or of the relevant reassessment of a principle previously known to that person.

Real history, in its expression as a lawful process, will therefore come, sooner or later, to destroy any form of human society which rejects that inherent mission. The penalty for any society's supporting the perversion shared among Gore and Princes Philip and Charles, would be awesome.

The consequence of the argument which I have just summarized, thus, here, is that man is distinguished so from the beasts, by this *noëtic* principle of the existence of the individual person.

All competent insight into the principles of a physically successful organization of the behavior of nations, is derived from the notion of human individual creativity as the uniquely original discovery of the universal principle of gravitation of the Solar System was discovered, as Albert Einstein emphasized, by Johannes Kepler.

The Theologian's View of Economy

This is not a theological argument in the simple-minded sense of matters; but, it does have a basis in what was, rather famously, the condemnation of the Aristoteleans by that friend of the Christian Apostle Peter known as Philo of Alexandria.

The argument of the Aristoteleans to whom Philo referred, is that those Aristoteleans were arguing in favor of Satan (whether they intended that or not) when they read the opening chapter of *Genesis* as suggesting that the Creator had finished his work, as being perfected, once the successive steps outlined in that chapter had been completed by Him. The Sophistry employed for that interpretation, was that, if the Creation had been perfect, the Creator Himself could not have altered what He had already created! Unfortunately, this scheme provided opportunities for the play of what were to be considered by theologians as agencies, such as the past and present forms of "malthusians," which would be unfriendly to God and man alike.

In short, the silliness of those Aristoteleans referenced by Philo, was that they demanded a God made impotent, his power of creativity terminated by his own actions! Philo left them with a devil of a time explaining that. The atheist who agrees with that Aristotelean, would nod approvingly: "Who should pray to an impotent Creator?"

The remedy for the Aristoteleans' silliness was, theologically and otherwise, that God's perfection is expressed as the view of a principle of a continuing power of Creation, a principle of universal anti-entropy expressed as a limitless sequence of phases of development to higher states of (anti-entropic) organization.

The sophistical objection to that from the Aristoteleans and their likenesses, was the argument attributed to the Olympian Zeus from Aeschylus' *Prometheus Bound*. The argument was that Satan (e.g., Zeus) would never permit mankind to practice a principle of anti-entropy: to be creative.

This was not simply an arbitrary rule. What Aeschylus identifies for us to be Zeus' domain, in *Prometheus Bound,* is the principle of empire which European history traces to the imperialism of an evil ancient Babylon. This was also the imperialism of the Roman Empire and of its successors. The rule of the imperialists, such as Diocletian (who, like Gibbon, would have preferred Julian the Apostate on this account), was, that the great mass of the human population, if permitted to exist at all, must live in dutiful submission to the rule that the ordinary man and woman must not seek to rise above his and her given station, but must adhere to the profession of his father. From the ancient *Iliad* through all Classical Greek tragedy, this evil rule of the gods serving Olympus was of this Babylonian type, a type traced from a degenerated mode of the Sumerian, so-called "hydraulic," bow-tenure culture.

In decent modalities in modern European society, the effect of scientific and technological progress is to be regarded as the proper destiny of progress from laborer, to skilled artisan, to machine-tool designer, to scientist, and, from farmer to modern scientific farmer operating in a relatively capital-intensive mode.

The Sarpi Legacy Today

If there ever were an actual Mephistopheles of Christopher Marlowe's and Goethe's fancy, he were certainly a suitable model for Venice's Paolo Sarpi. The model explicitly adopted for this purpose, by Sarpi, was that systemic irrationalism of the medieval William of Ockham. Ockham's irrationalism was adopted by Sarpi as the unifying basis for all of the dogma of Anglo-Dutch Liberalism, up through the present day.

I summarize now what I have presented in numerous locations published earlier. I caution the reader at this point, that the argument to be supplied here, while inescapable in any practical treatment of the subject of modern economy and so-called "geo-politics," is very tricky ground for discussion. My difficulty here does not lie in any fault I should attribute to myself, but in the confusion which the popularization of the Anglo-Dutch Liberal dogma of Ockham has embedded in contemporary academic and related life. This impediment to accepting reason is especially notable in the special relationship which Ockham's influence has shown in the cases of both the frankly anti-scientific positivism of Ernst Mach, and the even more radically Ockhamite dogma of Bertrand Russell and his followers since the publication of Russell's ***Principia Mathematica***.

Today, few victims of contemporary higher academic education have escaped what is fairly described as "brainwashing" in the sheer lunacy promoted by followers of Russell devotees such as Professor Norbert Wiener and John von Neumann.

Creativity in presently known physical science, since the ancient Pythagoreans, has depended essentially on the notion of the meaning of what modern practice identified, not as imaginary, as the Eighteenth-Century reductionists proposed, but, as the, ontologically, efficiently existing, Leibnizian *infinitesimal*.

This idea, as it had been treated previously extensively by Nicholas of Cusa and his followers, such as Johannes Kepler, focuses on the exemplary case of Kepler's demonstration of the existence of *the ontologically infinitesimal* as the expression of efficient principles which do not correspond to the human images of naive sense-perception, but are nonetheless efficiently demonstrated, as gravitation is, to exist as efficient effects of a universal character. *As Albert Einstein's emphasis on the validity of Kepler's genius should remind us: We can not see the universe which encloses our existence as an object of sense-perception; but, we must respectfully acknowledge the actuality of that universality's effects.* The case of Kepler's uniquely original discovery of the general principle of gravitation which corresponds to the organization of the Solar System, is, as Albert Einstein emphasized centuries later, a demonstration of the existence of universal physical principles which efficiently bound action within a universe which is therefore finite, but not externally bounded.[12]

These discoveries represent efficient ideas, which can be willfully demonstrated to be such by mankind, but which appear to the human senses, as in Einstein's praise of Kepler, as if *ontologically infinitesimal*. This latter notion was introduced to the founding of modern science by Nicholas of Cusa, who was followed explicitly on this account in the development of modern science by such exemplary individuals as Leonardo da Vinci, Kepler, Fermat, Christiaan Huyghens, and Gottfried Leibniz.

The Principle of Experiment

The notion involved, is, simply stated, the fact that our given senses are comparable to scientific instruments, in the sense that no one of these provides the mind a direct sense of the real universe. It is through discovering the paradoxes posed by comparing the co-incident experience of different qualities of senses, or different qualities of laboratory instruments co-deployed paradoxically, as surrogates for sense-perception, that the human mind itself is impelled to go to a higher level than mere sense-certainty, to discover the reality which is not the bare evidence of any of these senses or instruments. The experimental proof-of-principle of such a discovery of a higher order than sense-perception, is the proper notion of an *idea*. Kepler's uniquely original discovery of universal gravitation, as recounted in his ***Harmonies***, which produced the only competent, modern notion of the principled organization of the Solar System, is an example of this.

All that are properly identified, thus, as experimentally demonstrable ideas of the real universe beyond the limits of sense-perceptual accuracy, such as the entirety of sub-optical microspace, exemplify the domain of the action properly known as the power of human individual creativity which is the only efficient proof of man's distinction from the beasts.[13]

That illustrative case, so identified, is also the key for the definition of the human individual creativity which sets the individual human being apart from, and absolutely above all lower forms of life. These considerations just so presented here in summary, are key for proper insight into the pernicious implications of the influence of the Ockhamite dogma of Sarpi on the typi-

---

12. That universe is, therefore, to be described as "self-bounded." The origin of this as a modern conception, is to be traced from Nicholas of Cusa's rejection of Archimedes' quadrature of the circle. That rejection features not merely the irony of point, curvature, and some apparent, ultimate line. It is demonstrated by Kepler even in his *The New Astronomy*, from the implications of curved motion shaped by a dynamic principle of equal areas, equal times. Also, see not only the opening two paragraphs of Bernhard Riemann's 1854 habilitation dissertation, but also the concluding sentence of that publication.

13. For a relevant illustration of this, see the LaRouche Youth Movement study of Kepler's work (https://science.larouchepac.com/kepler/newastronomy/part4/60/index.html). Consider that body of work on file from the working standpoint of the LaRouche PAC website's video *Harvard Yard* (https://youtu.be/wSk3OIrhDfA).

cal failures of putatively scientific thinking today. In other words, the inability to comprehend this referenced discovery of universal gravitation by Kepler, as that discovery was later upheld by Albert Einstein.

The notion of underlying physical values, for the purpose of economic analysis, must reflect these considerations.

Sarpi's argument, as presented by such among his school's followers as the empiricists de Moivre, D'Alembert, Leonhard Euler, Lagrange, Laplace, and Cauchy, has, as I have noted above, denied the existence of the relevant ontologically infinitesimal, as de Moivre, D'Alembert, Euler, and their followers did, as "imaginary." Accordingly, they do not identify universal physical principles as such, but employ a chosen substitute in mathematical formulas, formulations whose significance is that those formulations are never better than the poor, adumbrated shadows cast by the actual physical principle expressed experimentally.

Seeing this incompetence of those Eighteenth-Century and later empiricists and positivists, is crucial for the competent understanding of those issues of physical economy which underlie all competent assessments of the matters of functions of pricing.

However, this is no mere matter of interpretations. It is precisely within the ontological domain which those Eighteenth-Century empiricists derided as "imaginary," that the factor of human individual creativity in economy is located *ontologically*.

Economy's Ontological Paradox

As a matter of principle, all net technological increase in the productive powers of labor in society, is dependent upon the kind of inventive mental activity which is typified by an individual's application of an experimentally valid notion of a universal physical principle of that class which the indicated, silly Eighteenth-Century empiricists derided as "imaginary."

At the same time that this consideration must be brought into play, the economy is experiencing attrition in the relative productivity of previously established technologies. The quality of what might be termed "customary resources" is suffering effects of attrition, at the same time that the increase of relative population-density defines a lower density of what current practice regards as customary resources per capita, per square kilometer.

Thus, progress, even maintenance of previous standards of output per capita, requires greater density of resources, and new qualities of resource combined, in effect, with more densely rich technologies.

Naturally, there is something which some of the Eighteenth-Century empiricist economists, and Marx came to recognize as the effects of depletion. Marx referenced the published work, *Riflessioni sulla popolazione delle nazioni per rapporto all'economia nazionale* (Reflections on the population of nations with respect to national economy; Venice 1790), of that Venetian economist Giammaria Ortes from whose English translation the Haileybury School's Thomas Malthus promptly plundered the essentials of his own, infamous *On Population*. The earlier precedents for that line of argument which has become synonymous with "Malthusian," are traced to the "proto-Malthusian" decrees of the Roman Emperor Diocletian. The appearance of the forerunners of "Malthusianism" in modern Europe is usually dated to Giovanni Botero's association with the thinking of the circles of Paolo Sarpi.

While Karl Marx did recognize aspects of the role of scientific and technological progress, he never understood this subject-matter in terms of scientific principles of physical economy. In fact, he confessed, in what is called Volume I of his *Capital,* that this involved a branch of economics which he was not addressing at that time. Indeed, the Soviet accomplishments in practice of science and technology, were more a product of the tradition of Russian physical science since the influence of Gottfried Leibniz and of the Freiberg Academy on Czar Peter the Great, than Marx. Marx, did not recognize a science of physical economy, and the Marxists generally were hostile to the notion of a science of physical economy of the sort we, today, would associate with the discoveries of Academician V. I. Vernadsky in the field of a science of physical chemistry which shared the field with scientists such as Chicago's famous Harkins.[14]

On the Subject of Pricing

The most significant of the recent decades' experiments in the domain of managing market prices, was the U.S. experiment with "fair trade" during the 1950s and the 1960s under President Kennedy. The U.S.A. coming out of the 1930s economic recovery from the 1920s and its Great Depression, and then confronting the austerity measures required by the conduct of World

---

14. A closely related problem came to the surface in a 1994 public debate with my friend Pobisk Kuznetsov, in the matter of the so-called "Second Law of Thermodynamics."

LaRouche has prescribed "long-ranging cooperation in development among sovereign nation-states," to produce large-scale capital improvements typified by great projects in basic infrastructure. Shown: the Shanghai, China maglev system.

War II, recognized that a certain degree of regulation of prices, called a "fair trade" policy, must be tested; that a turn to a "free trade" policy would be ruinous, as the terrible error of "free trade" has been demonstrated, even violently, in the world's persisting decadent movement toward a general, presently global breakdown crisis of today, since August 1971.

The actually productive sector of the U.S. economy had always been committed implicitly to a "fair trade" policy in the approach to tariffs and kindred measures of policy-shaping. The expressed thinking of Franklin, Hamilton, Mathew Carey, and Henry C. Carey is exemplary. President John F. Kennedy was continuing the exploration of management of "fair trade" policies during his conflict with the steel magnates, and in the design of taxation policies designed to encourage corporate reinvestment in long-term capital improvements. The Franklin Roosevelt recovery and the experience of World War II had taught us some useful lessons, despite President Harry Truman.

The outcome of those and kindred developments reached a relative high-point of good approximation under President John F. Kennedy. What followed has been catastrophe, a presently global catastrophe.

Where the Future Takes Us

If we assume, as I do for the purposes of this report, that we are at a point of desperately hopeful opportunity for all mankind. We are, thus, on the verge of establishing the form of long-ranging cooperation in development among sovereign nation-states which I have prescribed, such that the greatest increases in categories of production globally will occur in very-large-scale capital improvements typified by great projects in basic infrastructure. These will be, to a very large degree, international projects of cooperation among sovereign nation-states, including projects whose initial development and turnover will span several or more generations.

The development of high-density and very-high density sources of power, the process of increasing the rate of flow of fresh, clean water through the world's national economies, a progressive revolution in the practice and principles of public health, very large-scale mass-transportation of passengers and freight emphasizing magnetic levitation, the development of new conceptions of raw materials and their processing, and increased emphasis on exploration of nearby space for scientific purposes, will lead the list of undertakings. These types of great undertakings will be the drivers which define the direction of organization of all leading phases of production.

These great projects will then define the base-line of capital factors underlying all significant other economic activity in the economies within and among nations of the world as a whole.

From this point of departure, we shall obtain the base-line of costs and values which will underlie and permeate all phases of production, trade, and consumption throughout the world. That base-line, tied to a fixed-exchange-rate system shared in common by respectively sovereign nation-states, will then define the base-line to be referenced in determining suitable levels of pricing and related cost-estimations among the cooperating national economies of the world.

Within that framework, individual freedom to innovate will be promoted, and will be actively present in precisely the degree that the potential scientific and relatively creativity of the individual person is promoted.

A "fair trade" policy requires that we rid our financial accounting practices of the corrupting traditions of usury. Shown: "Christ Driving the Moneychangers from the Temple," an etching by Rembrandt (1635).

4. Why a 'Fair Trade' Policy?

> *3. The absence of a scientifically competent standard for defining "earned" profit margins, a standard needed to rid the current practice of financial accounting of its corrupting traditions of usury.*

The general principles of what have been known, in earlier times, as "fair trade" policies, have been indicated in the immediately preceding chapter. However, as in discussing diet, it is not sufficient to emphasize what is beneficial; it is urgent that there also be a warning against more or less deadly poisons.

Therefore, the essential point, stated summarily, is that there is no statistical or comparable convergence of "market-driven" determination of prices on relative economic values, whether that matter is as discussed by followers of the doctrine of Karl Marx, or not. That is the lesson which should have been recognized by any actually competent economist who has considered the patterns of the relations of volumes and relative prices over the course of the recent four decades of, in particular, North American and European trends.

It is nonetheless possible, of course, and, sometimes, also useful to compare trends in prices with contrasted physical-economic data. When this is done properly, it has the usefulness of showing up the fact that movements of prices may reveal some awful blunders in policy of economic practice (they often help to show us the patient—the economy—as sick), but neither temperature-readings, nor series of prices are reliable, in themselves, as indicators of the medicine required.[15] Cures of most kinds of very bad current forms of long-term economic trends, lie in the domain of practice of physical economy, as was the case for the U.S.A. during the 1939-1945 interval of general warfare in the world, when sundry controls balanced with military requirements had to be considered in light of the conditions of warfare.

For example, following the death of U.S. President Franklin Roosevelt, it was increasingly commonplace to hear that there had been something wrongful about pricing polices under the conditions of the 1941-1945 interval of the U.S. engagement in the general warfare of the 1939-1945 interval. On the contrary, if we acknowledge that price controls and related arrangements were necessary for the winning of that war, the price structures under that war-time regimen were closer to fulfilling both the current and future developmental requirements of physical reality than at any time later.

For example, the post-war intention of the Franklin Roosevelt Administration, was to convert much of the 1939-1945 wartime build-up of production for warfare, into non-military production for development of the peace-time world economy, including the freeing of what had been colonial territories. The cutting back of much of this potential, rather than realizing it through useful development in the world economy, made it dif-

---

15. As in the three sets of measures I have prescribed for the U.S.A.'s required measures under conditions since July 2007 to present date.

ficult to deal with the accumulated war-expenditures debt of the U.S.A. during the post-war years.

In a different case, in the contrary effects seen during the costly 1964-1975 interval of U.S. warfare in Southeast Asia. In the latter case, the lack of correlation between prices and physical values, was increased radically from U.S. Fiscal Year 1967-1968 onward; this discrepancy was accelerated, from that point onward, by the sharp cut-backs in net growth, even replacement of basic economic infrastructure during the latter part of the 1960s, and beyond.

As the developments of the 1960s demonstrated, veteran planners of serious warfare, qualified military officers, such as Generals of the Armies Douglas MacArthur and his former aide Dwight Eisenhower, showed then that they are usually far better economists, in practice, than the typical accounting specialists of today, as the case of Defense Secretary Robert McNamara has demonstrated.

In general, the notion that medium-to-long-term movements in relative prices converge, as if statistically, on appropriate relative (e.g., "market") values, is one of the most popular, and most stupid ideas commonplace in the field of statistical economic forecasting. This convergence virtually never occurred under "free trade" conditions; throughout the 1971-2008 interval, the trend toward "free trade" has been an increasingly disastrous one.

The most successful, and most profitable periods of the economies of the U.S.A. and modern Europe, have been periods of great increases in ratios of indebtedness *on capital accounts, especially in government uttering of debt in the matter of public expenditure.* In other words, these have been periods of high rates of physical-capital formation, combined with high ratios of advances in productive and related technologies. These governmental actions include greater rates of investment in competent forms of scientific training and higher rates of Classical artistic education.

The key to such ironical patterns, is that the real economy functions, over the medium to long term, in response to physical conditions, rather than financial projections as such.

The happier periods of exceptionally high rates of growth of physical productivity per capita and per square kilometer, are also associated with high rates of net increase in the debt associated with rising ratios of physical-capital investment with rising rates of physical productivity per capita and per square kilometer of

national, or regional territory. This includes increased rates of so-called "public investment," as distinct from what is usually classed as "private investment."[16]

The entire span of that period of the U.S. economy since Fiscal Year 1967-1968, had been a process of what has been an overall net physical decline in the net physical productivity and average quality of full "life-span" of productive investment, during that period to date. This is illustrated by a net collapse, through attrition, in outstanding margins of basic economic infrastructure since Fiscal Year 1967-1968, since which there has been nothing but a net collapse of the basic economic infrastructure of the U.S.A. as a whole.

The worst effects came over the course of the 1970s and beyond, through the combined effects of deregulation and the wrecking of the real economy under the 1977-1981 Carter Administration's implementation of the Trilateral Commission's program of the intrinsically highly inflationary method of controlled disintegration of the U.S. economy.

This attrition has been more or less concealed, fraudulently, by a gradual elimination of the accounting practices of national economic accounting which used to emphasize the proper, functional distinction between current and capital budgets. If the commitment to maintain public capital budgets which are sufficient to maintain what had been the capital invested in public infrastructure at parity levels per capita and per square kilometer had been enforced, there would have been no significant long-wave of rising real deficits in the public infrastructure budgets on which the Rockefeller Foundation's accomplices now seek to prey.

This element of accounting fraud introduced to the post-1971 practice of U.S. national accounting, was reflected in effects felt in the domain of physical productivity. For example: the high point of *the rate of* scien-

---

16. So-called "ppp's" (public-private partnerships) are echoes of the practices of the fascist regime of Italy's dictator Benito Mussolini, and are, by nature, intrinsically an integral feature of a predatory, fascist form of economy and nation-state. Notably, the principal argument of the Rockefeller Foundation, which has taken a leading position, together with New York's Mayor Bloomberg, in promoting the fascist "ppp" program, has been the failure of the Federal and state governments to maintain previously existing levels of infrastructure during the 1968-2008 interval to date, a wrecking of the U.S. economy done in the name of promoting "free trade" advantages for private investors! Now, they propose to turn over the infrastructure already created on public account, to the worst among the private financial predators which have plundered the economy in ways which brought much of our publicly maintained infrastructure into its present state of relative ruin.

The high point of the rate of scientific progress associated with the U.S. space program was reached by 1967-68, at which point savage cutbacks were introduced into aerospace and related research and development programs. As a result, the ability to complete the intended Moon Landing program was being used up, by attrition, with each of the successful flights launched during the early 1970s. Shown: The Apollo 16 launch, April 16, 1972.

tific progress associated with the U.S. space program was reached by Fiscal Year 1967-1968, at a time when savage cut-backs were introduced into the related research and development programs associated with aerospace and related programs.[17] It is a truism to suggest that, therefore, the ability to complete the intended Moon Landing program was being used up, by attrition, by the U.S. Administration, with each of the successful flights launched during the early 1970s. That certainly is the view of the recent forty years in retrospect, today.

That space program had been, by its inherent nature, among the most efficient generators of profitable forms of investment in scientific and technological progress

of the period since the program had been launched. During the 1970s, there was an estimate of a ten-cent return to the economy, on this account, for every penny advanced for space-program R&D.

This same historical-economic consideration appears when we are willing to see the ridiculousness of the suggestion that urgent military requirements necessarily require a cutback in physically capital-intensive investments in relevant general agro-industrial and infrastructural programs. History demonstrates the opposite conclusion. It is the increase of the technologically progressive productive powers of labor of society as a whole, per capita and per square kilometer, especially in industrial and agricultural labor and basic economic infra-structural capabilities, the which is essential support for all programs essential to missions such as warfare or any great program of progress.

The increase of the productive powers of labor, per capita and per square kilometer, means an increase in the ratio of physical-capital accumulation in categories of scientific-technological advances relative to general consumption otherwise.

On these accounts, every trend in U.S. technological-economic orientation of policy introduced since 1967-68, has been, in effect, more clinically insane, and more damaging than its predecessor. We have the results to prove that, in any honest examination of the physical-economic history of the U.S.A. during the recent forty years. The worst physical-economic damage done to the U.S.A. and its citizens during those forty years of ruin, have been policies oriented to promotion and toleration of recreational drugs, and to what is called, euphemistically, the kind of "environmentalism" associated with such worshippers of that Satan called the Olympian Zeus of Classical tragedian Aeschylus' ***Prometheus Bound***, as Britain's Princes Philip and Charles, and their American patsy, that lying, pro-genocidal, pro-bestial fanatic, former Vice-President Al Gore.

The characteristic of the human species, especially

---

17. Some wags might object, "But, buddy, there was a war on." The reply to such an objection would have been, "Buster, if President Kennedy had not been shot, then, the cronies of Defense Secretary Robert McNamara would not have been able to bring us, fraudulently, into that particular war." Former Prime Minister Blair's fraudulent means employed to bring the U.S.A. into the current warfare in Southwest Asia, is a notable example of the point. We have been destroyed, now, as then, by wars launched on such fraudulent pretexts. Indeed, one of the most effective ways to destroy a foolish once-great power, such as our own, is to permit that power to buy into lies like those of McNamara's and Blair's crowd.

of that species' progress from pathetically primitive conditions, has been the increase of our species' potential relative population-density, an increase accomplished only through the equivalent of the increase of the potential relative population-density of national cultures generally. We are, by given nature, a progressive, future-oriented species. *We live, and progress, not by re-arranging the proverbial deck-chairs of policy, but by the way in which we choose, or fail to choose, and commit ourselves to our advances into the future.*

Therefore, there is no idea more efficiently inhuman, than the idea that the standard for human economic behavior should converge upon some asymptote associated with a previously established level of practiced technology. Civilized society is governed by a devotion to generating the progress of the future now, not an obsessive occupation with re-enacting, and depleting the practices of the past. *Capital-intensive modes of development and investment in scientific progress are required; this commitment to increasingly capital-intensive progress, is, thus, the emblem of the expressed difference between human beings and the beasts.*

The Roots of Imperialism: a Synopsis

The world is presently menaced, chiefly, by two institutions of policy-shaping. First, the failure of most governments and peoples of the world to understand the nature, and origins of the present form of a British empire dating from about A.D. 1763 to the present instant. Second, the actual nature of that empire, rather than the presently popular fairy-tales on that general subject. Chancellor Otto von Bismarck knew better, so they dumped him.

To understand the monstrous threat of a new world war today, we must proceed from the understanding of the actual, rather than popularized mythical view of the matter of that British Empire which came into being as the imperial power of the followers and heritage of Paolo Sarpi, that in the form of the private, financier-oligarchical form of the British East India Company, a power secured during the proceedings of the February 1763 Peace of Paris: a triumph of the British power which had organized and steered the so-called "Seven Years War" for precisely that purpose. That Company itself has dissolved into the rotting woodwork of its past, but the spirit of that Company lives on, and reigns today, as the principal past and present foe of the existence of that U.S.A. which London presently infests as a parasite penetrating virtually all of the U.S. Repub-

lic's financial, political, and cultural institutions, as it also corrupts those of most of continental Europe as well.

While it is widely conceded that the British Empire emerging from the imperial maritime power of the British East India Company, has been, essentially, a maritime power, from even before the beginnings of its imperial power in the outcome of the Seven Years War, the unfortunate fact is, that most of the world's present governments conceal the true nature of their principal foe, the actual British Empire, from themselves, by refusing to look behind a mask which is the fading, comi-tragic trappings of feudalist pomp of the present, decadent British monarchy.

Those observers miss the essential fact, that the British Empire always was, as it is today, essentially a financier oligarchy in the Venetian tradition, specifically the Anglo-Dutch Liberal tradition of Paolo Sarpi. This is the essential truth which is displayed with full rottenness by that modern petroleum "spot market" established, chiefly in concert with Saudi Arabia, through an international petroleum swindle of the early through middle 1970s.

The Mediterranean Roots

This development of that real-life British empire of today has ancient Mediterranean roots, the roots of the empires relatively familiar to relevant historians who have examined the world's history since about the time of the alliance of the Etruscans, Egyptians, and Ionians, against the tyranny of Tyre, since about the Seventh Century B.C. The tracing of the development of those roots to the present-day form of the British Empire, is absolutely indispensable for understanding the remedy for the general economic-financial breakdown-crisis which has seized our entire planet today.

The birth and continued existence of that empire has a history. Unless that history is understood as a pathologist must examine a disease, the infection can not be effectively defeated. Therefore, some essential notations must be supplied by me here.

What is properly defined strategically as a fairly well known form of European culture, emerged from earlier arrangements at some time during the Seventh Century B.C., when the Egyptians (as also represented by Cyrenaica), entered into a working alliance with the Etruscans and Ionians, for mutual defense against the predatory Mediterranean maritime power of Tyre. Indeed, the roots of European culture are to be traced to the effects of earlier trans-oceanic maritime cultures (from which we obtained what became our best ancient calendars) which colonized the coastal and lower riparian regions emerging from the seas, in the aftermath of the millennia-long melting of the preceding, long glaciation in the Northern Hemisphere, in particular.

The appearance of the scientific method known as the *Sphaerics* of the Pythagoreans and Plato, typifies the earlier origins of the notion of "universe" in the astronomy of great navigational cultures. Thus, the dominant cultures under which European culture emerged, were the maritime cultures which tended to colonize the relevant lower riparian and coastal sites of the Mediterranean, especially from about the time a great freshwater lake was invaded from the Mediterranean, to form what we call today "the Black Sea." Thus, it was the most advanced cultures, the maritime cultures, including the culture of Egypt which had the same general maritime origins, which dominated the emergence of what became European civilization.

Because of the transoceanic cultures' access to the science of the "universe," through study of the astronomical changes essential to trans-Atlantic navigation over many centuries and longer, it was from this origin and continued development of the best known ancient calendars, that the essential foundations of scientific capability were developed by mankind.

The Homeric **Iliad**, dating from a relatively late phase in this Mediterranean process, has long been a point of reference to some significant cultural aspects of the emergence of a maritime-culture-dominated development of the Mediterranean and related regions of Europe, near Asia, and northern Africa during the First Millennium B.C., until Cardinal Nicholas of Cusa's proposal for trans-oceanic outreaches inspired Christopher Columbus, from about A.D. 1480, into what became the trans-Atlantic colonization of the Americas from Europe and northern coastal West Africa, from A.D. 1492 on.[18]

Thus, the emergence of the Mediterranean maritime culture of Europe, especially the more familiar period since the Seventh Century B.C., is crucial for insight into the emergence of the influence of maritime culture in shaping the evolution of today's globally extended

---

18. The times of great maritime cultures of China prior to Europe's Fifteenth Century, and Leibniz's identifications of the related ancient development of astronomical science in China, are comparable matters of historical concern for those intent to gain a better understanding of mankind for today.

European history since such ancient times.

Thus, the relevance of bringing those matters up here. I explain the connections now.

Trade & Imperialism

The economic advantages of maritime cultures over inland cultures, have persisted from ancient times, until the U.S.A. introduced the concept of the development of the trans-continental railway system. An approximation of this latter development had been introduced under Charlemagne through the building up of a relevant network of streams and canals in France and eastward, a developmental process which was still actively in progress into the 1990s. In both the U.S.A. and in Europe, the development of national, continental, and transcontinental railway systems based upon the development of the steam locomotive, tended to lie along existing riparian and canal routes of traffic in freight.[19]

Notably, the destruction of the continental railway system, and its replacement by highway transport, has been an intentional, London-centered, geopolitical trick for wrecking of the U.S. economy, rather successfully, during the recent fifty-odd years.[20]

It had been, in turn, earlier, under the influence of the development of transcontinental railway systems inside the United States, especially since the international impact of the 1876 Philadelphia Centennial exposition, that transcontinental railway projects of continental Eurasia were launched in Bismarck's Germany and under the guidance of the universal scientist D.I. Mendeleyev in Russia. This specific development, on both sides of the Atlantic, was already the origin of the new policy of the British Empire under the growing influence of Prince of Wales Edward Albert, to destroy both the United States and continental European powers such as France, Germany, and Russia, by what became

---

19. The development of the steam-engine was originally sponsored by Gottfried Leibniz, while the development of the efficient general use of the steam-engine involved discoveries organized in Britain and France by Franklin, Priestley, and collaborators such as Watt. This was, as documented by my associate Anton Chaitkin, the American initiative which organized the beginnings of the industrial revolution inside England— largely from the colonies in North America, as in the case of the Saugus Iron Works in Seventeenth-Century Massachusetts.

20. During the last years of the 1950s, I worked up a plan for rationalization of the national railway freight transport, beginning with the integration of the Pennsylvania and New York Central systems, through the creation of a computerized initial transfer and storage facility in the northern New Jersey area. This reform died on Wall Street, with the sad outcome clearly visible today.

The economic advantages of maritime over inland cultures, prevailed, from ancient times, until the U.S.A. introduced the concept of the development of the transcontinental railway system. Shown: Russia's Trans-Siberian railroad, modelled on that of the U.S.

known as two "World Wars" of 1914-1917 and 1939-1945, as also the Prince's inciting and aiding Japan in the launching its great, recurring war against China and Russia—and, then the U.S.A.—over the interval 1895-1945.

This continuing warfare-in-fact, by the British financier-oligarchical Empire-in-fact, against the U.S.A. and continental Eurasia, over approximately the span 1876-2008, is the key to tracing the ins-and-outs, twists-and-turns of British operations against the U.S.A. and other relevant targets, including Britain's intended victims on the continent of Europe today. That is the significance of the British monarchy's use of the foolish former U.S. Vice-President from Possum Hollow as the neo-Malthusian puppet of Princes Philip and Charles, and of Britain's George Soros of the World War II period's notoriety in the mass murder of about a half-million Jews, for Soros' more recent role in extensive British Foreign Office not-so-covert operations against targets in many parts of the world, as in the recent developments in Georgia.

As we can plainly see in retrospect today, since the first election of the wretched Harold Wilson as Prime Minister, the British empire has shown virtually no present interest in actually producing much of anything; it trades, following the trail of all usurious parasites who suck the blood of humanity in buying cheap, and selling dear, as Lord Shelburne's other American-hating lackey, Adam Smith prescribed.

The development of that British Imperialism other-wise known as the Anglo-Dutch Liberalism of the present-day heirs of Venice's Paolo Sarpi, has reached the point of seeking to establish a truly naked form of global imperialism of the type prescribed by the overt fascist H.G. Wells, and Wells' crony Bertrand Russell of "world government through preventive nuclear war" notoriety.

Already, as under the bestiality of the WTO, the British empire in its present form has gone to such grotesque postures as showing what is intended to pass for moral indignation against any nation which attempts to resurrect the almost dead tradition of national sovereignty, any nation which attempts, thus, to resist the British empire's insistence that anything you produce in your own nation you must not be permitted to consume, and everything you consume must be paid for at dear prices which are highly profitable to the middle-man, the British Empire, which supplies such foreign-made products obtained by the British from labor-intensive sources at cheap-labor prices.

At the same time, the British system, acting according to the whims of such predators as Princes Philip and Charles (with Al Gore tagging behind), makes clear that these WTO policies are intended to assist London's intention to reduce the world population, by the means proposed by the late Bertrand Russell, from over six-and-a-half billions persons on this planet, to no more than two, and that in considerable haste in the making.

One might ask: Is there any proffer of pretended rationality about these clearly Brutish imperial demands? In the meantime, while one were waiting for the answer to the question concerning their method for bringing that result about, the fact is already clear, that Princes Philip and Charles are intent on the early achievement of their stated population and related goals. For all of which, they are expected to be regarded with great respect, even, perhaps, reverence.

Empire's Ancient Motive

None of this brutishness from those quarters is novel in known ancient, medieval, or modern European history. This is the tradition of all expressions of true European imperialism, and the Babylonian tradition, too. After its close cousin, prostitution, imperialism is among the oldest of institutions, and diseases, known today. The relationship of prostitution and the like to imperialism is most simply expressed by the close relationship of both to, and abundant liaison with the systems of money. In other words, monetarism as we know it from such examples, runs along the pathway down to the nearby port, from that cult of Delphi where the treasuries of the notable worshipful cities surround the temple. In other words, the center of the practice of the usurious racket which Plato had intended to have shut down.

All of the ancient European empires which have existed since that time, have been based on the control of the valuation of money in the closely related practices of simple usury and international trade. The premium placed on controlling the pathways of navigation and related matters, so that this control may be established over the difference in money-price between buyers and sellers, has been the most profitable function of what had become modern trade under WTO conditions today. The purpose of WTO rules is to establish the greatest achievable margin of marketable difference, and distance, between "cheap" and "dear."

It is that kind of control over international or kindred forms of trade, which has always been an essential constitutional feature of monetary functions of any actual or would-be empire.

The mechanism of control depends upon the existence of another, complementary feature of the system of imperialism: the Olympian pagan religious (Gaea-Python-Apollo, or Apollo-Dionysus) cult of Delphi, as that was echoed in the function of the Pantheon of ancient imperial Rome. The most essential features of such intrinsically tragic cult-mechanisms are the subsuming subject matter of the Homeric *Iliad*. The great tragedian Aeschylus used the ancient Egyptian account of the Atlantan chronicle of the Olympian Zeus' conflict with Prometheus, to open the secrets of European imperialisms to his audience for the story of the ***Prometheus Bound.***[21]

The crux of the matter was, and remains, the banning of knowledge of "fire"—meaning such things as nuclear power today—from the knowledge of ordinary men and women. In the Prometheus account, "fire" is generic for that human individual creativity by means of which individual persons discover universal physical principles.

London & The Drug Trade

Thus, during the Nineteenth Century, the British Empire had used the Spanish monarchy as the handmaiden of its dirty work in the same African slave-trade used as a lever of the British imperial crown in the effort to create the Southern states' slavery system intended to enable the British to destroy the United States by aid of such penetration. The British, who had abandoned direct trafficking in African slaves during the 1790s, had turned the slave-trade over to their agent, the Spanish monarchy, so to conserve British vessels for the vastly more profitable opium-trade which, today, is still funding Saudi, Afghan and other investments in the vastly profitable illegal, international traffic in opium and its derivatives around the world. Then, as today, it is the British empire which actually controls the bulk of this trafficking. They engage in their part in managing this traffic not only for obvious profit-margins, but as a weapon of subversion used against sections of the populations of targeted nations.

Thus, as the case of London's George Soros illustrates this point, the Anglo-Dutch Liberal financier interests abandoned the work of appearing to conduct the narcotics trade, by limiting their own visible role largely to the imperial political, as much as the direct financial profits. This has been typical of imperialism since long before the British Empire existed.

Today, since the role of the so-called "68ers," the following related factors have been in play in assisting the British Empire in the work of eliminating the United States and some other nations which are too important to be overlooked as targets. The creation, from among a "systemically white collar" sector of the U.S. and European persons born between 1945 and the 1958 midpoint of the first major U.S. economic recession, of future adult youth who were "pre-programmed" by the obvious methods of targeting "White Collar" and "Organization Man" households of that period, to become the wildly irrational, enraged, Dionysian stratum of "blue collar-hating," science-hating "68ers" of the late 1960s and 1970s. One is reminded of that academic, Friedrich Nietzsche, dying and rotting of venereal disease in a foul attic, when one thinks of those 68ers now.

This stratum of haters of science, of industrial and

---

21. At a later, Roman time, the Sicilian chronicler Diodorus Siculus gave an account which he attributed to the then-contemporary descendants of the ancient Berbers.

of agricultural development, and of Classical culture generally, became the notorious "White Collar" shock-troops of the political establishment between about fifty to sixty-five years of age inside the U.S.A., most of western and central Europe, and relevant other parts of the world today.

It were sufficient to read the literature of the latter sociological phenomena of mass-politics today, to recognize the kind of "mass-brainwashing" which the policies of the Olympian Zeus' ban on knowledge of "fire" represent for the world's politics and economy today.

Unfortunately the victims of that "brainwashing" which we must associate with the hard-core of the leading political layer drawn from the same cultural matrix as the "68ers," have dominated the cultural trends among the ruling political strata of government and economic life today. This layer typifies the most concentrated expression of those cultural types of victims of Zeus-like "brainwashing" in the leading political strata of Europe and the Americas today. This is the hard-core constituency of imperialism in the world at large today, especially within northern Europe and the Americas, but not limited to those areas.

Economics & Creativity

Refer back to the review of the role of human creativity in defining the absolute nature of the difference between ecology and economy.

The source of all net physical growth in the productive powers of labor, even the ability of society to prevent an attritional slide into the decadence of too long spent doing nothing better than the same old thing done in the preceding generation, depends upon that quality of the human mind lacking in all lower forms of life.

So, the history of past empires, and the lurking fate of the British Empire and its "neo-Malthusian" lackeys of today, is the attritional effect of attempting to sustain a human population over a long time according to the Delphi Apollo-Dionysus tradition implied to be that of the Olympian Zeus. The attempt to establish and maintain a relatively powerful empire, results in a depletion in the kinds of resources which the relatively stupefied population conditioned to a fixed level of technology prefers. At a certain point, the doom of that society becomes inevitable. Then, out of that catastrophe, some echo of the old ruling ways starts the attempted build-up of imperial power, and this is repeated, over and over again, with, or without a Julian the Apostate. Such is the history of empires in general, and the empires since the fall of the Achaemenid empire in particular.

Now, the population of the planet has reached the level of more than six-and-a-half billions living human individuals. That population can not continue to exist under the conditions prescribed by the British Empire and its accomplices of today. Hence, we have heard the suggestion that the planet must now suffer the catastrophe of a collapse of population from more than six-and-a-half billions persons, to level of two or less. Perhaps Philip thinks himself to be Julian the Apostate; at least he tries out for the part.

Scientifically, probably no institution in existence today could fairly estimate where bottom would be if Prince Philip's ambition were tolerated, but, bottom would be, actually far, far below a level of two billions humans. We hover, thus, at the brink of a catastrophe which simply must not happen. The remedies are two. First, the British Empire must be brought to an end. Some replacement, like the idea of the peaceful cooperating, sovereign nations of Ireland, Scotland, Wales, and England, would be a sensible alternative. Second, we must uproot every trace of the influence of imperialism, while reorganizing the population of the planet as composed of respectively sovereign nation-states committed to sharing the promotion and use of the available new technologies which lie beyond nuclear-fission power as such. That change would not be an end, but only a needed beginning. Above all, in all this, it is the development of the creative powers of each society's human individuals in a world, which must have eradicated everything from its policy of practice which looks like, or smells like the agenda of former U.S. Vice-President Al Gore.

---

5. Vernadsky & Economy

4. The failure to bring the notion of economy up to date, scientifically, in terms of the notions of Biosphere and Noösphere.

The most common fault of which I know in studying the thinking processes in society, is the inability, or, worse, in the refusal to recognize that that human creativity which distinguishes man from beast, is essentially personal. "Let's be objective" can usually be relied upon as an indication that the person who introduces that suggestion is either about to lie, has just lied, or is simply feeling very uncomfortable about the direction in which the deliberation is proceeding. Perhaps it is because he, or she has something to hide. Or, perhaps, it is because he, or she fears that either his or her own ignorance of the subject at hand is about to become manifest. Sometimes, however, for reasons which I illustrate here, that involves an important issue of scientific method.

That resistance is of a quality typified by the situation in one member of a group is showing signs of irritation with the course the discussion is threatening to take, as if that person fears that things may be about to come up in the course of that discussion, which would indicate such a thing as the existence of a secret mistress to persons who either know the person's wife, or the man's mistress.

The expression such latter person might employ is, "Let us get off that subject!" What is actually in danger of being revealed, is not so much the identity of the man's mistress, but, as, in scientific, or certain other matters, how the speaker's mind actually works.

For example, often, in my working experience as an economist, or in political-intelligence matters, someone has suspected that I "must have received" information he had preferred that I not know, or not be able to reveal. Often, the fellow feeling such a concern, has simply failed to grasp the point that I, for example, am responding to nothing but what he himself had just inadvertently revealed. In relevant cases, the source of his error of assessment is essentially his lack of the quality of creative insight essential for scientific method. There are people who, therefore, deeply resent, or even hate, those others who are able to "see things," such as matters of scientific principles, which their blocked mind will not, or does not wish to see. They hate that as much, or more than the revealing of the identity of a secret mistress.

This syndrome is, or ought to be notorious in the field of scientific work generally. By the nature of the social character of the subject of economy and its principles, the type of problem to which I have referred leads quickly to angry outbursts within the discussion of matters of principles of economy, especially when the discussion borders on someone's, such one of today's financial speculator's, fear of losing his, or her accustomed, or merely desired right to steal.

I explain the crucially important point toward which I am pointing with that illustration, by using those immediately preceding remarks as a way of referring to a very personal, and crucially important aspect of scientific method, as follows.

Science & Personal Insight

Out of respect for the limited access to certain physical resources, sometimes available to me in those particular settings, I have concentrated my principal life's effort, overall, to the subject of the outcome of my fortunate devotion, since early adolescence, to a certain kind of an expression of human creativity, an outlook typified by my good fortune, since adolescence, to have recognized the implicit evil of the promotion of Euclidean geometry and related methods.

That piece of good fortune brought me to a consequent, agreeable association with the legacy of Gottfried Leibniz, and, onward from that, to the implications of Bernhard Riemann's 1854 habilitation dissertation. However, it had an important added consequence of great specific relevance to the matter of physical economic science with which we are dealing in this report.

In the course of time, in the immediate aftermath of my admittedly modest war-time service and its experience, the experience from my adolescence and early adulthood, was combined with an incurable stubbornness in resisting anything which, so to speak, "smelled" like more reductionist sort of academic, or comparable pablum, even when the subject-matter was otherwise intellectually attractive. This steered me into emphasizing a commitment to the idea of human creativity as such. This was stimulated, as my experience overall had shown me repeatedly, by my discovery, about myself, that what I detested the most was that which I became most passionately impelled to dissect and cure. Thus, the relevant output of Professor Norbert Wiener, John von Neumann, and their patron Bertrand Russell, became such targets, although scarcely the only such, which I could not relinquish. Thus, my adult professional experiences, and similar matters, purified my focus into one of concentration on the subject of creativity *per se*.

By the late 1950s, my fascination with the problem of the lack of creativity in business executives and management consulting personnel, in particular, drew my attention to some work by Dr. Lawrence Kubie, a work with which I came to disagree on certain points, but found nonetheless fruitfully challenging. Later, I appreciated very much a message relayed to me from Kubie: *Creativity is itself intrinsically a good.* It was not a new idea for me, in any degree, but hearing it stated so by one whose work I had studied in connection with my own professional practice, my spirits were much refreshed by hearing that message.[22]

Creativity as such is not only a good in its own right. It is the true essence of that which sets the human individual apart from, and above the beasts. Virtually all persons have this quality, as an intrinsic distinction of their share in human nature, but, today, in only a very few does that potential survive the social conditions to which individuals are usually subjected, even in the nations which are most generously endowed with access to knowledge.

What pleases me most in my own experience and development along those lines, has been cracking the virtual wall which separates the individual's access to knowledge in physical scientific matters from the principles of Classical artistic composition, especially in the matter of the non-plastic arts. That matter of the conventional separation of the one department of creative efforts from the other, is a subject with which I have associated for about sixty-four years since the impact of what I experienced in reading Percy Shelley's *In Defence of Poetry*. I bring the discussion now, thus, to the point of these opening paragraphs of this chapter of the report,

Mathematics Versus Science

It has become, unfortunately, customary in modern education and along related tracks, to identify scientific creativity with formal mathematics. As I recognized the mistake of that customary belief, I also recognized that the proof of my objection should have been obvious. That is, in any creative discovery of a solution in principle for a viciously perplexing paradox, the typical problem is that the nature of the answer to the paradox

"Not only has Vernadsky led a great and profound revolution in understanding ourselves and our relationship to the universe we inhabit, but very few, even scientists, so far, have grasped the more fundamental ontological implications of his contribution." Academician V.I. Vernadsky, in 1940 photo.

has a certain proximity to mathematical forms of expression, but that expression is never better than a shadow cast by the relevant conception generated in the mind.

The scientific treatment of Kepler's uniquely original discovery of the principle of gravitation includes several crucial illustrations of this point, as does the work of Fermat contributing to the principle of least action, the discoveries of Leibniz, and so on.

Essentially, all valid expressions of creativity as such, share this characteristic. The discovery of a true physical principle, as Johannes Kepler demonstrated this so powerfully in his *Harmonies*, or, any great performance of a Classical musical masterpiece, demonstrates that there is a correct reading of the Beethoven (for example) score, but, as Wilhelm Furtwängler both argued and demonstrated, it "lies between the notes."

As I have referenced this point earlier in this report, any actual discovery of a universal principle must, by its very nature, "lie between the notes," as Kepler's uniquely original discovery of the principled character of the orbit rests on the discoverer's flash of insight into the existence of what I have fairly described as an *ontological infinitesimal,* the infinitesimal expression of a principle which envelops, rather than being enveloped by the principle which contains the relevant

---

22. This message passed to me from Kubie was notable because he was not only a leading psychiatrist of that time, but, nominally at least, a Freudian. As I have referred to such matters in some of my work published during the 1970s. there are some isolable outbursts in Freud's published work on the subject of society as such, which tend in the direction of Kubie's message, but Freud's attachment to the mechanistic influence of Ernst Mach is all too notable in his work as a psychiatrist. Kubie's emphasis was relatively unique, formally and morally. With that I concurred with his argument, especially as he situated it with respect to pathological factors arising in what had been otherwise promising scientific minds.

action: i.e., which bounds the action, as Albert Einstein's universe is an expression of a finite, but, ontologically, infinitely self-bounding principle.

The folly of the introduction of the notion of "imaginary" magnitudes by de Moivre and D'Alembert, illustrates the point.

Think of a sterile strict reading of the intention lodged behind the literal performance-reading of a score by J.S. Bach or Beethoven, and we realize that that intention does not allow liberties, but, as in the case of the distinction of a mathematical formulation, ontologically, from the principle to which the formulation refers, performance of great Classical musical composition, as in the legacy of such as Leonardo da Vinci and Johann Sebastian Bach, requires a more demanding precision than the mere score itself could show. When we accept the relevant evidence of that, then, we have gained an insight, which Kepler, doubtless, would enjoy. That insight is: that the actually creative occurrence of ideas specific to, respectively physical science and Classical musical performance, are ultimately of the same nature. The only real difference, is that, in physical science, the subject is man acting upon the universe; whereas, in the irony intrinsic to Classical artistic composition, as by Bach, Mozart, and Beethoven, or Leonardo da Vinci, earlier, it is the mind of man acting upon the mind of man in social processes, as its subject.

The problem with all such and related matters of the relationship of human creativity to irony, is, that, so few people today have not lost most of even the powers of creative insight which were not entirely uncommon during the 1950s, the insight needed to make such ideas, the ideas which inhabit the domain of specifically human creativity, their own.

The importance of saying what I have just stated thus far in this chapter, is that it expresses the hope of improving the access of people to the natural power of creativity within them, a power which could be greatly improved by aid of willful means.

The discovery of a true physical principle, as Johannes Kepler demonstrated this so powerfully in his Harmonies of the World, *or, any great performance of a Classical musical masterpiece, "lies between the notes." Kepler, in a 1610 portrait.*

Poetry, For Example

Since Classical poetry, when it is actually poetry of which Keats and Shelley would not be ashamed, is the closest sibling of Classical music, I have come to the conclusion, which you may regard as merely heuristic, if you wish, that a certain course of experiencing the evolution of competent physical science along a pathway from Pythagorean *Sphaerics*, through Cusa, Leonardo, Kepler, Fermat, Leibniz, Gauss, and Riemann, that in the setting of the blending of the relevant Classical prosody and manifest benefits of Florentine and related *bel canto* voice-training, is probably the most effective choice of pathway for promoting what Kubie identified as promoting the quality of scientific creativity which we are failing to promote in leading university programs today.

The more I digest the kind of argument which I attribute to what I suspect have been believable translations of Vernadsky's work from the last decades of his life, the more important I consider the standpoint which I have recommended for approaches to a more or less universal standard for higher education today. It is also clear, that not only has Vernadsky led a great and profound revolution in understanding ourselves and our relationship to the universe we inhabit, but that very few, even scientists, so far, have grasped the more fundamental ontological implications of his contribution.

Please assume that I might have now repeated everything I said in the preceding paragraphs of this chapter, but this time from the notions of Biosphere and Noösphere as a context of physical-economic reference.

The Crucial Implications

In all competent appreciation of Classical artistic composition and valid modes in fundamental scientific progress, the ontologically infinitesimal, as I have described it during the course of these pages, reigns supreme. Call it "mind over matter," if you wish. The power of the human mind which is lacking in all beasts, is not merely a difference between man and beasts; in our respective ways of functioning, we and the beasts live *as if* in different universes. The universe as only man could know it, rather than the beasts, is not only the real universe, but our actions as incarnated personalities are actions within the domain experienced by the beasts, but the beasts do not know this. The difference is that our species is defined, as if by the Creator, as like the man who runs the zoo within which the animals are kept. It is our actions, on this account, actions of which the beasts are not capable, which define our essential, functional relationship to the universe as a being made in the image of the Creator.

The problem is that people, for the most part, see themselves, in most moments of their living, as more in the likeness of the beasts, than their Creator. This is shown, chiefly, in the fact that most people, even those aware of the actual presence and function of human individual creativity, think of creativity as if it were a kind of magic which intervenes from outside our real existence. The tendency to see matters in those terms, is strongly re-enforced by the social fact of today, that most of the human beings with whom we are associated do not actually believe in the existence of true creativity, and therefore do not seek to define their social relations in terms of creativity as a human characteristic of man as a social being.

They, even most of the actually creative people, tend to locate their personal identity in the part of themselves which dies, rather than in terms of those social relations we share with those departed and also with the yet to be born. Generally speaking, it is only those of us, such as creative scientists and Classical poets, who are in an active, efficiently productive quality of practical intellectual relationship with the principles adopted by deceased important thinkers of the past, who find in that fully efficient, if immortal quality of efficient social re-

Experiencing the evolution of physical science, from Pythagorean Sphaerics, through Cusa, Leonardo, Kepler, Fermat, Leibniz, Gauss, and Riemann, combined with Florentine bel canto voice-training, is probably the most effective way to promote the quality of scientific creativity needed today. Shown: two panels from Luca della Robbia's "Cantoria" (1430s), in the Florence Cathedral.

lationship in the form of a dialogue with minds from the past, the effect of what we sense as "cathexis" with those relevant minds living in the past. In theology, this quality of efficient social connection with past individuals, is classed under the heading of "simultaneity of eternity." Let the deceased smile in our imagination when we think of them in this way.

No truly competent scientist, nor any competent professional, or knowledgeable audience for great Classical musical composition, is ignorant of that quality of connections with creative work which is radiated into the present, from past generations. It is impossible to understand Beethoven, or any of his compositions, except as he is engaged in a dialogue with Bach and Mozart, among others. It is not because those subjects are "old," that we revere them; it is because they represent the experience which has defined the materials of the work with which we must begin to act now.

When you can experience the impulse to shout across time, "Franz Liszt, as a composer, you are the terrible faker that Beethoven warned that that criminal Czerny would cause you to become!" "All those pianos at Wahnfried! All squatting like sleeping, elephantine dinosaurs. What an awful spectacle of waste!"

All competent pursuit of physical science occurs as a dialogue spanning no less than the lapse of time since the Pythagoreans.

Those who adopt the profession of making history, of which competent practice of science is typical, must *live the relevant past as an active presence within themselves, as really a living part of their presently immortal identity with respect to both future and past.* Otherwise, they will make a horrible mess of things, as the present generation of leaders in Europe and North America, for example, have done of late.

Then, Consider Vernadsky

Vernadsky's establishing the concept of the Biosphere, when this aspect is combined with his more primitive, but provisionally valid insight into the principled nature of the Noösphere, has, in a manner of speaking, "changed everything" for the scientist, or statesman who has grasped what Vernadsky has actually accomplished.

Rather than seeing the human species (ourselves) as popped up like a toaster-tart from the Earth we inhabit, we experience the progress from inhabitants of what they might have been assumed to have been popped-into as a given environment, to the experience of the development of our bodies from the preceding evolution of the materials of us which do not die, but which have been assimilated to form the bulk of those materials of which our living bodies are composed to form us, not as a species of animals, but as in the likeness of the Creator.

However, there is nothing of spontaneous generation in this process. We are not made of inorganic materials, as if we had been creatures molded from clay. If you must have analogies, if they will be of any assistance, consider your body as a recording medium, in which it is merely the imprint of your development which dwells. The medium decays, but what is experienced may be replicated in other ways, as within, for example, the medium of society as a whole.

At this point in this report, certain debts must be, so to speak, paid.

Put that point in other terms, as follows. Start with Vernadsky's definition of the Biosphere. What really convinced me that the argument of Vernadsky, which I already considered important, was to a certain degree conclusive, was, ultimately, my good fortune to be associated with Chicago University Professor Robert Moon, who was, himself, a particularly accomplished former student of the great physical chemist William Draper Harkins, whose work must be associated in physical chemistry with the role of D. I. Mendeleyev, as in opposition to the reductionism of the notable British reductionist schools. The effect of my own association with Professor Moon crystallized into a more important relationship around the implications of Vernadsky's discoveries in a certain fashion, during my vigorous defense of the work of Kepler against the frauds of Newton, during several general meetings of the leading body of the Fusion Energy Foundation. My argument prompted Professor Moon to return to some uncompleted work of his own in physical chemistry. The lines of work which this prompted were crucial for situating lines of inquiry of continuing relevance for today.

That coincidence of the legacy of Professor Harkins' leading role in Twentieth-Century physical chemistry with that of Academician Vernadsky's treatment of the physical chemistry of the Biosphere, when that is viewed appropriately in retrospect by us today, has a basis in authority which reaches far beyond issues of physical chemistry as such, into the higher realm of the means of experimental validation specific to the domain of the science of physical economy, my own field.

There is an essential universal principle here. To understand the universe, we must start from the top down, with mankind, rather than, as is, unfortunately customary, from the bottom up (where, in fact, it usually remains). As an effect of the validation of Academician Vernadsky's discoveries in physical chemistry, our comprehension of the place of man in the universe has been implicitly transformed, lifted to a higher plane than mankind has known, ever before. The standpoint required to appreciate these implications of Vernadsky's accomplishments, in light of this and related developments, is the conception of the immortality typified by the cases of truly great minds, which is common to great Classical artistic composition and the essentially non-mathematical aspects of fundamental scientific progress in the heavenly potential for the improved condition of mankind in a domain of the simultaneity of eternity.

The necessary, if introductory argument for this case, can now be stated from the vantage-point of the implications of Vernadsky's contributions. I summarize that argument here, as I do, because what must be discussed between us and relevant Russians today, under the presently given considerations of a global existential crisis of all mankind, is the ecumenical task of finding the underlying common cultural denominator which will be capable of binding the U.S.A., Russia, China, and India, together as a keystone of a system among the respectively sovereign cultures of many nations.

It was very good that Cardinal Mazarin and others established that 1648 Peace of Westphalia to which all truly civilized persons on both sides of the Atlantic adhere still today. "To love one another," is a sound principle; but, it is not sufficient. There must be a higher ranking mission which binds differing cultures together in an impassioned devotion to a common end, an end which can not be mere peace among peoples, but some

"I have devoted my principal life's effort to the outcome of my fortunate adolescent devotion to an expression of human creativity which is typified by my good fortune to have recognized the implicit evil of the promotion of Euclidean geometry and related methods," LaRouche writes. Here, LaRouche gives a class to his associates in Leesburg, Va., July 1985.

purpose which binds them, even among different faiths, passionately, to a common outcome.

The statement required could be uttered in theological terms, and probably shall be presented so. Unfortunately, the state of relations among putative and equivalent religious beliefs is not particularly good. For the good of all, let us, for the moment say it in my fashion.

The Thesis

The crucial feature of the standpoint from which to trace the social implications of Vernadsky's combined treatment of the Biosphere and Noösphere, is the inescapable implications of the interactions, as in both physical science and Classical artistic composition, of the efficiently active personal relationship between the thinker living today and the thinker living even thousands of years earlier.

Out of respect for the extremely limited physical resources sometimes available to me during the past, I have devoted my principal life's effort to the outcome of my fortunate adolescent devotion to an expression of human creativity which is typified by my good fortune to have recognized the implicit evil of the promotion of Euclidean geometry and related methods. This brought me to the consequently agreeable association with the legacy of Gottfried Leibniz, and, onward from that, to the implications of Bernhard Riemann's 1854 habilita-

tion dissertation.

In the course of time, in the immediate aftermath of my war-time service and its experience, the experience from my adolescence and early adulthood, combined with an incurable stubbornness in resisting anything which, so to speak, "smelled" like more reductionist sort of academic pablum, even when the subject-matter was otherwise attractive. This steered me into a commitment to the idea of human creativity as such. This was stimulated, as my experience overall had shown me repeatedly, by my discovery about myself that what I detested the most was that which I was most passionately impelled to dissect and cure. The relevant output of Professor Norbert Wiener, John von Neumann, and their patron Bertrand Russell, became the targets, although scarcely the only such, which I could not relinquish. My adult professional experiences, and similar matters, purified my focus into concentration on the subject of creativity *per se*.

By the late 1950s, my attention to the problem of the lack of creativity in business executives and management consulting personnel, in particular, drew my attention to some work of Dr. Lawrence Kubie, with which I came to disagree on certain points, but found his work a fruitful challenge nonetheless.

As I have already emphasized above, in my references to Dr. Lawrence Kubie, creativity as such is not only a good in its own right. It is the true essence of that which sets the human individual apart from, and above the beasts. Virtually all persons have this quality, but in very few does that potential survive the social conditions to which individuals are usually subjected, even in the nations which are most generously endowed with access to knowledge today,

What pleases me most in my own experience and development along those lines, has been cracking the virtual wall which separates the individual's access to knowledge in physical scientific matters from the principles of Classical artistic composition, especially in the matter of the non-plastic arts. That matter of the conventional separation of the one department of creative efforts from the other, I have associated for about sixty-four years with the impact of what I experienced in reading Percy Shelley's **In Defence of Poetry**. I come, thus, to the point of the opening paragraphs of this chapter of the report,

It has become unfortunately customary in modern education and along related tracks, to identify scientific creativity with formal mathematics. As I recognized the mistake of that belief, I also recognized that the proof of my objection should have been obvious. That is, in any creative discovery of a solution in principle for a viciously perplexing paradox, the typical problem is that the nature of the answer to the paradox has a certain proximity to mathematical forms of expression, but that expression is never better than a shadow cast by the relevant conception generated in the mind.

Essentially, all valid expressions of creativity as such have this characteristic. The discovery of a true physical principle, as Johannes Kepler demonstrated this so powerfully in his *Harmonies*, or, any great performance of a Classical musical masterpiece demonstrates that there is a correct reading of the Beethoven (for example) score, but, as Wilhelm Furtwängler both argued and demonstrated, the truth of the composer's intention "lies between the notes."

As I have referenced this point earlier in this report, any actual discovery of a universal principle must, by its very nature, "lie between the notes," as Kepler's uniquely original discovery of the principled character of the orbit rests on the discoverer's flash of insight into the existence of what I have fairly described as an *ontological infinitesimal,* the infinitesimal expression of a principle which envelops, rather than being enveloped by the principle which contains the relevant action: i.e., which bounds the action, as Albert Einstein's universe, is a finite but infinitely self-bounding principle.

The folly of the introduction of the notion of "imaginary" magnitudes by de Moivre and D'Alembert, illustrates the point.

Think of a sterile strict reading of the intention lodged behind the literal performance-reading of the score by J.S. Bach or Beethoven, and when we realize that intention does not provide liberty, but a more demanding precision than the score could show, we have gained an insight, which Kepler, doubtless would enjoy, that the actually creative occurrence of ideas specific to, respectively physical science and Classical musical performance, are ultimately of the same nature. The only real difference, is that in physical science, the subject is man acting upon the universe; in irony intrinsic to Classical artistic composition, it is the mind of man acting upon the mind of man as its subject.

The problem with all such and related matters of the relationship of human creativity to irony, is that so few people today have not lost most of the powers of creative insight needed to make such ideas, the ideas which inhabit the domain of specifically human creativity, their own.

The importance of saying what I have just stated thus far in this chapter, is that the hope of improving the access of people to the natural power of creativity within them can be greatly improved by aid of existing willful means.

Since Classical poetry, when it is actually poetry of which Keats and Shelley would not be ashamed, is the closest sibling of Classical music. I have come to the conclusion, which you may regard as merely heuristic, if you wish, that a certain course of experiencing the evolution of competent physical science along a pathway from Pythagorean Sphaerics, through Cusa, Leonardo, Kepler, Fermat, Leibniz, Gauss, and Riemann in the setting of the blending of the relevant Classical prosody and *bel canto* voice-training, is probably the most effective choice of pathway for what Kubie identified as promoting the quality of scientific creativity which we are failing to promote in leading university programs today.

The more I digest the kind of argument which I attribute to what I suspect have been believable translations of Vernadsky's work from the last decades of his life, the more important I consider the standpoint which I have recommended for approaches to a more or less universal standard for higher education today.

Please assume that I might have now repeated everything I said in the preceding paragraphs of this chapter, but this time from the notions of Biosphere and Noösphere as a context of physical-economic reference.

Our Dialog Among the Immortals

As every qualified scientist or Classical artist knows (otherwise, they are not qualified), the practice of one's profession reaches across many generations of the departed, to an intimately personal, and active relationship across a span which usually reaches as far as some thousands of years. Unfortunately, most of contemporary popular art reaches back no further that the depths of mud, or some less pleasant antecedent. Similarly, the fraudulent teaching of physical science prevalent in universities and other places today, abandons everything from the past which is not either pathologically mythical, such as the intrinsically incompetent work of

Isaac Newton, or sufficiently disgusting to please the appetites of popular entertainments. François Rabelais, like Boccaccio before him, or Miguel Cervantes (if few among the latter's present-day readers) would understand.[23]

In the mind of the accomplished Classical artist or scientist, the spirit of such worthy departed (and also some other) souls are in our presence as if still living, and that virtually either within the same room, or on some telephone connection or comparable arrangement. We argue with these departed. We breathe a living spirit into their works, and seek actual evidence which would point out to us what their response might be to our question, or in objection to what we are thinking.

Consider my following examples minted to illustrate the point to which I am leading here. Become prepared to view the work of Vernadsky from this same vantage-point.

Take the case of the remarkably good somewhat short story of Stephen Vincent Benet, **The Devil and Daniel Webster**, which some among us would consider in the spirit of typically New England stuff. Or, consider the featured videos recently produced for LaRouche PAC by my associates of the LaRouche Youth Movement (LYM) as practical demonstrations of the same principle. Consider these compositions as informed by the experience of bringing the actual process of discovery of the foundations of a competent modern science to life, in the LYM work on the discoveries of Kepler which supplied the foundations of a competent modern astronomy.

It is within the framework of that *simultaneity of eternity,* bringing the voices of the relevant deceased back as if to life in the dialogue of the present, in which truthful conceptions are set afoot among the minds of contemporary men and women. Silly people live in the present moment, a moment which will soon die; people who know what it is to be human, or possess at least an inkling of that, are never existentialists; they live within a dialogue of living and departed alike. It is that dia-

EIRNS/Elizabeth Mendel

The LaRouche Youth Movement's work on the discoveries of Kepler, which supplied the foundations of a competent modern astronomy, is bringing the process of discovery of the foundations of a competent modern science to life. Here, members of the LYM participate in a class on Kepler's Harmonies of the World.

logue that their knowledge of experience inhabits; it is in the active dialogue among the living and the relevant departed, that the meaning of the mortal life of a human being is really situated.

We must confess, that Stephen Vincent Benet did a brilliantly good job.[24]

Now, extend the principle of history so illustrated to our present relationship to the Biosphere, and also the abiotic domain.

Prior to the relevant discoveries by Academician Vernadsky, especially the consolidation of that work which developed from the mid-1930s onward, most of mankind enjoying the benefits of a modern European education, visualized mankind as if dropped from outer space upon the relatively habitable regions of our planet. We were, in that sense, and in that degree, more or less aliens within this habitat.

Prior to the work of Vernadsky, especially from the mid-1930s, onward, mankind as mankind, which is to say, not some variety of ape, had a relationship to our planet like that of visitors from outer space whose ancestors had colonized this planet. With Vernadsky's work, especially that from the mid-1930s onward, the

---

23. Spending the night chatting with a prostitute, is not, as Shakespeare's Doll Tearsheet could have explained, an uplifting occupation.

24. I.e., *The Devil and Daniel Webster*. The motion-picture version was not bad, either.

historical perspective of our species had been profoundly changed. We were now of this planet. It could not be assumed, by people with respectable scientific opinions, that life in general was a secretion of non-life. Once we compared mankind's population characteristics with those of the beasts, including the higher apes, we could no longer presume that mankind was simply an evolution of some animal species.

Going a qualitative step further than that, any serious examination of the nature of the variability of the potential population-density of the human species, showed that there was nothing attributable to the characteristics of any and all marsupial or mammalian species which could account for the way in which the developing of human cultures brought about the virtually willful increase of the potential relative population-density which occurred only through the kind of cultural development which the edict of the Olympian Zeus' ban on use of "fire" would have forbidden. So, our existence was thus distanced, qualitatively, from that of any, or all known forms of life.

The significance of these distinctions is made clearer by an examination of the demonstrable, "historical" changes in the relative masses of the products of the respectively abiotic, biotic, and cognitive contributions to the component residues of the outer regions of our planet. We are, thus, of this planet, and, as the Solar System is of the process known as our Sun, we are of this Solar System, and, implicitly, of the universe as a whole.

What I have just emphasized in the immediately preceding paragraphs now complements the simultaneity of existence of both our living and our deceased of all times thus far. This is a conception which is shown, functionally, to be a true conception of ourselves, and our heritage as a species in this universe.

In our essential nature, as what we might term the still tiny minority of the "relatively most enlightened" among us, we do, indeed, live in a simultaneity of eternity, as that view was expressed in Raphael Sanzio's "The School of Athens."

Cooper Consulting Co./J. Craig Thorpe

The pathway out of the awful predicament which menaces the human species today, is the rapid development of advanced economic infrastructure across the planet, centered on a keystone alliance of the four great powers, the U.S.A., Russia, China, and India. Here, an artist's conception of Bering Strait Railway Tunnel between Wales, Alaska, U.S.A. and Uelen, Chukotka, Russia.

The problem is, that most of the people of this planet do not yet see themselves in these terms, in terms of a notion of a simultaneity of eternity. That deficiency among our people is the principal source of the persistent, but remediable great evil which has plagued our species in all known times to date.

Epilogue: the U.S.A., Russia, China & India

Now, that much said up to this point, return to our starting-point of this report.

In viewing the awful predicament which, once again, menaces the existence of the human species on this planet, the considerations which I have selected for sampling in the preceding sections of this report, appear to be the only adducible remedy for the presently immediate threat of a general thermonuclear and related holocaust on this planet.

Since the most menacing features of the current strategic situation are chiefly a reflection of the combination of what the British Empire is, and what the United States of America, unfortunately, has failed to do in keeping faith with its own revolutionary tradition, it is necessary to recognize that the British Empire, which, in fact, is currently in top-down control of these United States, is the nearest approximation of a true representation of

Satan, as it was when it created Mussolini and Adolf Hitler as geopolitical strategic tricks earlier.

Yet, when we think more carefully about these matters, this evil which the British empire in its present form most precisely expresses, is less an evil in its own right, than an expression of what we of the United States, for example, failed to do when we had, formerly, the power, under President Franklin Roosevelt, for example, to prevent this presently perilous situation threatening all humanity. Evil is not as much a power in its own right, as much as it is the expression of the absence of the good.

What should capture our attention in viewing this presently perilous situation menacing all mankind, is the following leading facts of the present situation.

First, that without the role of the U.S.A. which I have prescribed, there is no hope for the assured continuation of civilized human life on this planet during generations yet to come. Second, the only partner presently available to the U.S. for this urgent mission is one other European culture, that of Eurasian Russia, and the leading Asian nation powers of China and India. There are other allies for this purpose, but the mission as a whole requires a firm commitment by the four indicated leading powers, whose actions will allow the others to enter as members of the same enterprise.

Second, all nations, including the indicated leading ones, must summon a relevant humility respecting the causes of this crisis of global humanity. It is the ignorance of the masses of poor, which has, in effect, disarmed the majority of the human race of the mental capability of organizing its own defense under these terribly perilous, global circumstances.

Thirdly, the essential problem is not merely that most of humanity, including its relatively wealthier, more privileged portions, is also a victim of the most corrupting of all moral disorders, not merely ignorance, but a defiant ignorance stubbornly defending the very ways which have been its complicity in its own oppression.

Finally, the most essential fault of humanity today, is its want of a competent sense of immortality of the person, not in the flesh, but in the simultaneity of eternity.

APPENDIX

FDR's Bretton Woods Plan

Here are excerpts from President Franklin Roosevelt's Feb. 12, 1945 message to Congress on the creation of the Bretton Woods system.

In my budget message of Jan. 9, I called attention to the need for immediate action on the Bretton Woods proposals for an international monetary fund and an international bank for reconstruction and development. It is my purpose in this message to indicate the importance of these international organizations in our plans for a peaceful and prosperous world.

As we dedicate our total efforts to the task of winning this war, we must never lose sight of the fact that victory is not only an end in itself but, in a large sense, victory offers us the means of achieving the goal of lasting peace and a better way of life....

If we are to measure up to the task of peace with the same stature as we have measured up to the task of war, we must see that the institutions of peace rest firmly on the solid foundations of international political and economic cooperation. The cornerstone for international political cooperation is the Dumbarton Oaks proposal for a permanent United Nations.

International political relations will be friendly and constructive, however, only if solutions are found to the difficult economic problems we face today. The cornerstone for international economic cooperation is the Bretton Woods proposals for an international monetary fund and an international bank for reconstruction and development.

These proposals for an international fund and international bank are concrete evidence that the economic objectives of the United States agree with those of the United Nations. They illustrate our unity of purpose and interest in the economic field. What we need and what they need correspond—expanded production, employment, exchange, and consumption—in other words, more goods produced, more jobs, more trade, and a higher standard of living for us all.

To the people of the United States, this means real peacetime employment for those who will be returning from the war and for those at home whose wartime work has ended. It also means orders and profits to our industries and fair prices to our farmers. We shall need prosperous markets in the world to insure our own prosperity, and we shall need the goods the world can sell us. For all these purposes, as well as for a peace that will endure, we need the partnership of the United Nations.

The first problem in time which we must cope with, is that of saving life and getting resources and people back into production. In many of the liberated countries, economic life has all but stopped. Transportation systems are in ruins, and therefore coal and raw materials cannot be brought to factories.

Many factories themselves are shattered, power plants smashed, transmission systems broken, bridges blown up or bombed, ports clogged with sunken wrecks, and great rich areas of farm land inundated by the sea. People are tired and sick and hungry. But they are eager to go to work again, and to create again with their own hands and under their own leaders the necessary physical basis of their lives.

Emergency relief is under way behind the armies under the authority of local Governments, backed up first by the Allied Military Command and after that by the United Nations Relief and Rehabilitation Administration. Our participation in the UNRRA has been approved by Congress. But neither UNRRA nor the armies are designed for the construction or reconstruction of large-scale public works or factories or power plants or transportation systems. That job must be done otherwise, and it must be started soon.

The main job of restoration is not one of relief. It is one of reconstruction which must largely be done by local people and their Governments. They will provide the labor, the local money, and most of the materials. The same is true for all the many plans for the improvement of transportation, agriculture, industry, and housing, that are essential to the development of the economically backward areas of the world.

But some of the things required for all these projects, both of reconstruction and development, will have to come from overseas. It is at this point that our highly developed economy can play a role important to the rest of the world and very profitable to the United States. Inquiries for numerous materials and for all kinds of equipment and machinery in connection with such projects are already being directed to our industries, and many more will come. This business will be welcome just as soon as the more urgent production for the war itself ends.

The main problem will be for these countries to obtain the means of payment. In the long run we can be paid for what we sell abroad chiefly in goods and services. But at the moment many of the countries who want to be our customers are prostrate. Other countries have devoted their economies so completely to the war that they do not have the resources for reconstruction and development.

Unless a means of financing is found, such countries will be unable to restore their economies and, in desperation, will be forced to carry forward and intensify existing systems of discriminatory trade practices, restrictive exchange controls, competitive depreciation of currencies, and other forms of economic warfare. That would destroy all our good hopes. We must move promptly to prevent its happening, and we must move on several fronts, including finance and trade.

The United States should act promptly upon the plan for the international bank, which will make or guarantee sound loans for the foreign currency requirements of important reconstruction and development projects in member countries. One of its most important functions will be to facilitate and make secure wide private participation in such loans. The articles of agreement constituting the charter of the bank have been worked out with great care by an international conference of experts and give adequate protection to all interests. I recommend to the Congress that we accept the plan, subscribe the capital allotted to us, and participate wholeheartedly in the bank's work.

This measure, with others I shall later suggest, should go far to take care of our part of the lending requirements of the post-war years. They should help the countries concerned to get production started, to get over the first crisis of disorganization and fear, to begin the work of reconstruction and development; and they should help our farmers and our industries to get over the crisis of reconversion by making a large volume of export business possible in the post-war years....

As confidence returns, private investors will participate more and more in foreign lending and investment without any Government assistance. But to get over the first crisis, in the situation that confronts us, loans and guarantees by agencies of Government will be essential.

We all know, however, that a prosperous world economy must be built on more than foreign investment. Exchange rates must be stabilized and the channels of trade opened up throughout the world. A large foreign trade after victory will generate production, and therefore wealth. It will also make possible the servicing of foreign investments....

A good start has been made. The United Nations monetary conference at Bretton Woods has taken a long step forward on a matter of great practical importance to us all. The conference submitted a plan to create an international monetary fund which will put an end to monetary chaos. The fund is a financial institution to preserve stability and order in the exchange rates between different moneys. It does not create a single money for the world; neither we nor anyone else is ready to do that. There will still be a different money in each country, but with the fund in operation, the value of each currency in international trade will remain comparatively stable. Changes in the value of foreign currencies will be made only after careful consideration by the fund of the factors involved....

[The whole package of measures] is our hope for a secure and fruitful world, a world in which plain people in all countries can work at tasks which they do well, exchange in peace the products of their labor, and work out their several destinies in security and peace; a world in which Governments, as their major contribution to the common welfare, are highly and effectively resolved to work together in practical affairs and to guide all their actions by the knowledge that any policy or act that has effects abroad must be considered in the light of those effects.

This point in history at which we stand is full of promise and of danger. The world will either move toward unity and widely shared prosperity or it will move apart into necessarily competing economic blocs.

We have a chance, we citizens of the United States, to use our influence in favor of a more united and cooperating world. Whether we do so will determine, as far as it is in our power, the kind of lives our grandchildren can live.

FIDELIO

Journal of Poetry, Science, and Statecraft

From the first issue, dated Winter 1992, featuring Lyndon LaRouche on "The Science of Music: The Solution to Plato's Paradox of 'The One and the Many,'" to the final issue of Spring/Summer 2006, a "Symposium on Edgar Allan Poe and the Spirit of the American Revolution," *Fidelio* magazine gave voice to the Schiller Institute's intention to create a new Golden Renaissance.

The title of the magazine, is taken from Beethoven's great opera, which celebrates the struggle for political freedom over tyranny. *Fidelio* was founded at the time that LaRouche and several of his close associates were unjustly imprisoned, as was the opera's Florestan, whose character was based on the American Revolutionary hero, the French General, Marquis de Lafayette.

Each issue of *Fidelio*, throughout its 14-year lifespan, remained faithful to its initial commitment, and offered original writings by LaRouche and his associates, on matters of, what the poet Percy Bysssche Shelley identified as, "profound and impassioned conceptions respecting man and nature."

Back issues are now available for purchase through the Schiller Institute website:
http://schillerinstitute.org/about/order_form.html

The Leaders of the United States, Russia, China, and India Must Take Action!

We, the undersigned, appeal to President Trump, President Putin, President Xi Jinping, and Prime Minister Modi, to convoke an emergency summit in order to create a New Bretton Woods global monetary system.

SIGN THE PETITION BELOW!

http://bit.ly/newbrettonwoods

Much of the world is in catastrophic disarray. There are acute dangers of a new financial crisis and of a potentially devastating trade war. The refugee crisis in the Mediterranean underscores both the plight of the people in Africa and Southwest Asia, and the disunity of the European Union. The demographic curve in the United States has taken an alarming downturn. For most ordinary citizens, it is very difficult to see how all these different problems can be efficiently addressed.

There is, however, only one fundamental cause for all these seemingly diverse crises. When President Nixon effectively eliminated the fixed exchange rates of the Bretton Woods System in 1971, American economist Lyndon LaRouche warned that a continuation of the monetarist policies that were introduced then, would inevitably lead to the danger of a new depression and a new fascism, unless a new, more just world economic order were created. In the wake of Nixon's action, there was a step-by-step deregulation of the financial system in the direction of neo-liberalism, which prevented the industrialization of the developing sector, and increased the profits of the speculators at the expense of the common good in the so-called advanced sector. The resulting systemic financial crisis of 2008 was not remedied by removing the causes of the crisis, but instead, the financial institutions of the British Imperial system acted to prolong the system of maximizing profits for themselves.

As Lyndon LaRouche has emphasized for many years, there is only one combination of nations that is powerful enough to replace this currently hopelessly bankrupt neo-liberal system, and that is an alliance among the U.S.A., Russia, China, and India. It would represent, by far, the largest political, economic, and military power, and thus be able to establish a New Bretton Woods System, in which sovereign governments control their own credit-creation, and can facilitate agreements among themselves to invest in the long-term development of infrastructure, industry, and agriculture for the benefit of the common good of their people.

The potential for such an alliance is very clear. China's Belt and Road Initiative has been instrumental in bringing about the emergence of a completely new economic system, based on "win-win cooperation" among more and more countries, leading to an incredibly rapid eradication of poverty in many of them. New organizations, such as the BRICS (Brazil, Russia, India, China, and South Africa) , the SCO (Shanghai Cooperation Organization), the EAEU (Eurasian Economic Union), and other regional organizations, are striving in the direction of a new economic order, based on the development of all.

While this may not be obvious to many, the American System of economy based on the principles of Alexander Hamilton, which President Trump has promised to reintroduce, has a great affinity with, and is based on the same ideas as the Chinese economic model and China's Belt and Road (or New Silk Road) Initiative. The leaders of Russia, China, and India have already stated their intention to cooperate on Belt and Road projects in Eurasia, Africa, and Latin America.

Once President Trump has been freed from the British coup known as "Russiagate," (which is now rapidly turning into a "Muellergate," and leading toward a criminal investigation of the perpetrators of the coup attempt), he will be able to deliver on his promise to put relations with Russia and China on a sound footing.

The only efficient way in which the many problems of the world can begin to be solved, is by the immediate establishment of a New Bretton Woods system—a new international credit system which makes it possible to increase the productivity of the labor force and to upgrade the physical economy. Once such a four-power agreement among the U.S.A., Russia, China, and India has been established, all other nations can join the new system, based on the principles of sovereignty and mutual respect for the differences in their social systems.

We, the undersigned, appeal to President Trump, President Putin, President Xi Jinping, and Prime Minister Modi, to convoke an emergency summit in order to create a New Bretton Woods System.

Will Brennan Be
Called Before a Grand Jury?

by Harley Schlanger

Aug. 19—The revocation of former CIA chief John Brennan's security clearance by President Trump should be recognized as the first step toward reversing the damage that he and his collaborators have inflicted on the United States. There are calls for a special counsel to investigate the "Russiagate" fraud that he launched with a guiding hand from the imperial forces of British intelligence. That campaign, which Trump calls a "witch hunt," has constrained the President from proceeding with a decisive break with the old geopolitical doctrine of confrontation with Russia and China—a doctrine fully embraced by Brennan during his career.

What Brennan launched, in the spring of 2016, was not just a witch hunt, but a regime-change coup, of the sort he often coordinated in the CIA. And while the Mueller investigation continues, the anti-Russian forces in Congress allied with Brennan, Clapper and other Obama intelligence chiefs, are aggressively pushing policies against Russia to prevent the possibilities for peaceful agreement.

EDITORIAL

The lifting of Brennan's security clearance was announced on August 15, with a press statement from President Trump charging that Brennan's "lying and recent conduct characterized by increasingly frenzied commentary is wholly inconsistent with access to the nation's most closely held secrets and facilities.... Mr. Brennan has recently leveraged his status as a former high-ranking official with access to highly sensitive information to make a series of unfounded and outrageous allegations—wild outbursts on the Internet and television—about this administration." (In addition to his hyper-active Twitter account, Brennan is a paid expert commentator for the anti-Trump network MSNBC.)

Brennan and his collaborators launched Russiagate during the presidential campaign, in an attempt to prevent Trump from winning the election. Brennan obviously favored the CIA-friendly candidate, Hillary Clinton, who worked closely with him in anti-Russia operations, as well as in the coup in Libya. Once Trump won, Brennan lied that "17 U.S. intelligence agencies" all agree that Russia meddled in the election on behalf of Trump—a claim he continues to make, without ever presenting any evidence (while only three, not seventeen agencies signed on to his charges). His most recent hyperbolic outburst was his attack on the Helsinki summit between Presidents Trump and Putin, in which he stated that Trump's "performance . . . rises to and exceeds the threshold of 'high crimes and misdemeanors.' It was nothing short of treasonous."

Trump's decision to revoke Brennan's security clearance triggered a barrage of vitriolic nonsense from Brennan and his allies. Former Director of National Intelligence James Clapper, a close ally of Brennan in creating the Russiagate narrative, who is also on the list of those who may lose their security clearances, called Trump's action an "infringement of First Amendment rights." Brennan himself offered evidence that this charge is bunk, when he authored an op-ed in the *New York Times* on August 17 headlined "President Trump's Claims of No Collusion Are Hogwash."

That this vile op-ed was published proves that Trump's actions do not infringe on his rights of free speech—only his right to receive classified briefings. But Brennan is not just exercising free speech in his attacks on Trump. He is continuing to coordinate the coup to remove Trump from office, largely on the grounds that he and his colleagues believe there can be no peace with Russia, and any effort by Trump to establish a productive dialogue proves that he is a "puppet" of Putin. It is Brennan who is a security threat to the United States, who has no inherent right to receive classified intelligence.

It is a sign of their "Trump Derangement Syndrome" that so many in the media and in the Congress jumped to Brennan's defense. During Brennan's time at the CIA, he committed multiple crimes: he covered up and then defended torture by his agency; he spied on Senate staffers investigating torture; he coordinated drone killings with Obama, including killings of American citizens, and hundreds, perhaps thousands, of civilians. And now, he is at the center of the web of lies and cover-up that characterizes the attacks on President Trump.

Brennan should be called before a Grand Jury to face these charges. But don't expect a proven, serial liar to come clean and tell the truth.